Where I Stand

Where I Stand

Volume II

A Collection of Speeches, Essays, and Newspaper Articles, 1995–1999

Papa Kwesi Nduom, PhD, CMC

iUniverse, Inc.
Bloomington

Where I Stand, Volume II
A Collection of Speeches, Essays, and Newspaper Articles, 1995–1999

iUniverse books may be ordered through booksellers or by contacting:

iUniverse
1663 Liberty Drive
Bloomington, IN 47403
www.iuniverse.com
1-800-Authors (1-800-288-4677)

ISBN: 978-1-4759-1047-6 (sc)
ISBN: 978-1-4759-1048-3 (hc)
ISBN: 978-1-4759-1049-0 (e)

Library of Congress Control Number: 2012906183

Printed in the United States of America

iUniverse rev. date: 04/03/2012

To my wife, Yvonne, who has stood firmly by me in difficult times and supported the use of my pen and voice to champion the cause of change for the greater good of the nation

Contents

Introduction

I n volume 1 of this series, I provided the reader some insight into how my views about Ghana and its future developed as the nation entered its Fourth Republic.

The period covered by this book, 1995 to 1999, is without a doubt the most difficult period of my life so far. It is the only period in my life when I confronted the fact of being Ghanaian and the difficulties associated with being a citizen and living in the country of my birth. From time to time during that period, I questioned why I remained a Ghanaian and why I wanted to live and work in Ghana considering all the challenges thrown at me by the party in power, the J. J. Rawlings–led National Democratic Congress (NDC) administration. I was even more disappointed by the actions of people I thought of as friends, some of whom had shared meals with me in my home several times. Others were employees and business colleagues who had benefited from opportunities I had given to them. They deserted me at the first hint of problems with the Rawlings administration. Senior business executives could not understand why a young man who they felt had a lot going for him could stray into matters dealing with politics and the way our country is run. Their advice was to "lie low" and enjoy business success quietly. That way, they counseled, the politicians would leave me alone. Interestingly, later, I saw some of these same people "stray" into the fringes of NDC or New Patriotic Party (NPP) politics. Even more disappointing is the fact that members of my own party, the Convention People's Party (CPP), used the trumped-up charges the NDC 1 administration tried desperately to pin on me later in 2007–2008 to discredit me and sabotage my campaign to become president of the Republic of Ghana.

I was shocked when a member of the ruling party told me when I complained to him in 1996 about the canceling of contracts without cause that, if they had been able to send thousands of public servants home through redundancy programs, why should they care if the few consultants I had lost their jobs. Even more shocking was when a top-level business executive canceled a multiyear contract my company Deloitte & Touche had with his company due to pressures from the administration. When I complained, all he said was he also had his problems.

But a few people stood by me and defended me vigorously. They were mostly associated with the *Ghanaian Chronicle* and *Independent* newspapers. Kofi Coomson, Kwaku Baako, Kabral Blay Amihere, Charles Wereko-Brobbey, and others in the media remained firmly on my side against the Rawlings administration's attempt to destroy my reputation and business interests. Others I did not even know that well back then were supportive. I owe them endless gratitude. But I also found out that many Ghanaian individuals, educational institutions, companies, and associations sought my company and asked me to speak at various events throughout the country. Some of those speeches are included in this document.

Also during the period, I became actively involved in politics in Ghana. Prior to this, I had been a member of a party and a supporter of candidates, but not an active player.

I

I remember when General E. A. Erskine (retired), Nana Okutwer Bekoe, and Mr. Mike Eghan came to my house to invite me to consider becoming the chairman of the People's Convention Party (PCP) and assist in uniting all those who considered themselves Nkrumaists. I told them that I was not ready and not well grounded enough in Ghana. This was prior to 1966. I should have taken the challenge back then.

The result of people using politics to attempt to destroy my businesses and send me to the Serious Fraud Office without just cause was my entry into active politics. I became determined to use politics to champion the cause of Ghanaian businesspeople, professionals, and ordinary people. I wanted to use politics to encourage our people to appreciate success. I have the Rawlings administration to thank for moving me from the sidelines of Ghanaian politics to center stage.

I chose to get involved at the grassroots level by seeking election to become an assembly member for the Akotobinsin Electoral Area, which included my home territory, Teterkessim in Elmina, to show how serious I was about public service. I campaigned from door to door and witnessed the shock on people's faces when they saw who was campaigning so vigorously, not to go to Parliament or become president, but to represent them at the local District Assembly. It was a smart move for me. I learned a lot and remain grateful that the people gave me the benefit of the doubt and voted me in with a landslide victory even though they were not sure what I was doing "down there." I began to appreciate what is meant by "a lot can be accomplished if we do not care who takes credit." My experience as an assembly member convinced me that, if the people are given the right to vote at the local level for their assembly members and district chief executives, they will make the right decisions and use the ballot box to ensure accelerated local development.

I have compiled these writings to show I have remained faithfully in the same place, "Where I Stand." The intensity of my desire is to see change that improves the standard of living of the ordinary Ghanaian in a significant way. I want this to happen in my lifetime. The failures of successive NDC and NPP administrations to unite the country and use their stay in government for a giant forward march gives me the energy to continue to be active in politics while I at the same time also use the private sector to provide jobs to those who my companies can employ.

So read for yourself and judge whether what I want for my country and its people has changed over the years or not. I believe that public service is an honorable undertaking. It requires honorable, serious people to make it work. In Africa, to engage in public service requires supreme dedication, sacrifice, and, unfortunately, quite often getting dirt thrown at you.

II

In the most difficult periods, I knew I would be okay because I had a great legal expert who later became a justice of the Supreme Court, His Lordship Dr. Seth Twum, not to defend, but to point me in the right direction and encourage me to continue to do the right thing and believe in the power of faith.

Brought Back to Ghana

I left Ghana on January 17, 1996, flying toward Washington, DC. My mission was to make a presentation on business opportunities in Ghana at a conference organized by the Wharton African Students Association (WASA) at the prestigious Wharton School of Business in Pennsylvania.

I was to share the podium with top executives from American Express, Ford Motors Corporation, General Motors, Merrill Lynch, Chrysler, General Electric, Arthur Andersen, and others. Our assignment was to open a window to the world of business to black business school graduates and entrepreneurs. We were to be role models, sources of information, guides, councilors, and recruiters. I was scheduled to speak at the conference on January 20, 1996.

The flight landed in Washington, DC, on the afternoon of January 18. The minister of finance at the time, Hon. Kwame Peprah, was on the flight. I said hello to him and exchanged greetings and small talk about the situation in Ghana. Officials from the Ghanaian embassy in Washington, DC, met him on arrival, and they whisked him away through diplomatic channels. I went through the normal immigration and customs procedures. I received the usual welcome greeting from an immigration officer.

Then my world changed. My brother met me at the airport. If he had been a white man, I would have described him as looking pale. He looked worried and carried a news story published in the *Ghanaian Times* of January 18, 1996. In it, there was an announcement that I had been

5

sacked from the board of directors of the Ghana Airways Corporation. This was said to be due to an investigation into the activities of the State Enterprises Commission. While I was to learn later that I was not a specific target of the investigation, my wife and I were alleged to have engaged in activities serious enough to warrant mention in the *Times* story. I was also the subject of a *Ghanaian Times* editorial that disclosed their version of fees alleged to have been paid to me, along with other comments related to my involvement with the Commission.

I am not sure how I got home from the airport. When we arrived at my residence at Lake Barcroft in Falls Church, Virginia, I realized how busy the fax machine had been. A number of people had faxed several copies of the same story and editorial to me. I spoke to my wife and learned I had been sacked from the same Ghana Airways Board on Ghana Broadcasting Corporation Television as well.

Within twenty-four hours, all contracts that companies I was associated with held with organizations related to government were suspended, canceled, or on notice to be cancelled! I had arrived in Ghana at last!

This is not a story about the government of Ghana, the State Enterprises Commission, the *Ghanaian Times*, or the Serious Fraud Office. It is about coming home to Ghana. As a result of January 18, 1996, I have come to understand why some people believe "it is difficult to go back home again."

In 1990, I seriously thought about moving from the United States to Ghana. As a Young Pioneer, I was supposed to be one of the new Africans, groomed to take my place in the country Kwame Nkrumah led to independence imbued with a new African personality characterized by excellence, confidence, and self-respect. I had come from a CPP home. My father strongly favored my going to the University of Ghana's School of Administration over my going to the United States. To him, there was more pride in staying in Ghana. Perhaps he was worried that I might not come back after my studies if I went outside of Ghana.

The early 1970s was a good time to be black in a university in the United States. There were benefits to be gained from the struggles of the 1960s. Being an African was definitely in. Being from Kwame Nkrumah's

Ghana was a major plus. I was at home in the inner cities, Nation of Islam, Catholic Church, university campuses, and a number of White American homes with an international perspective. I was proud to be an African so much so that I promptly decided to use the Fanti name that my parents gave to me at birth instead of the European name I carried.

While I read everything I could find about African leaders, Malcolm X, Martin Luther King Jr., Elijah Mohammed, Marcus Garvey, and others, I joined a study group dedicated to mastering international business and commerce. We believed the future belonged to those who understood the world of finance. We subscribed to the thought that "the independence of Africa will be meaningless unless it is linked with economic prosperity."

I was without malice. I was without negative feelings of any type about Ghana. I did not know Kalabule, Unigov, June 4, or 31 December. I just wanted to take the resources I had gained in the United States and the experience I had gained as a Deloitte & Touche partner to come home to join in the fight for economic prosperity for the masses of our people. It turns out that other forces would pull in a different direction because, to them, my very existence in Ghana threatened their hold on power.

Many friends and relatives were not happy to hear about my intentions to come back to Ghana. Letters and telephone calls came to warn me about my "rash decision." Some wondered if I had lost my job in the United States. When it became clear that I was bent on coming home, there was a universal counsel. "When you go, stick strictly to business, and don't show anyone that you have money. If you are invited to chair any function, decline it politely. Stay away from government and the opposition. By all means, avoid harvests. Lose the American accent, and blend in. Stay out of trouble!"

I thought I was going home. It did not feel like it.

After January 18, 1996, I have learned a few lessons. I am even more fiercely committed to contributing to the building of a prosperous Ghana. I love being in Ghana. I am convinced that it is my duty as a beneficiary of Kwame Nkrumah's African Personality training to give some of it back to those who were not so fortunate and missed the positive part of being a Young Pioneer.

I still receive more than my share of advice to be careful and stay out of trouble. But I constantly ask myself when I drive by the rural areas and the poor urban slums: Can I live with myself if I am one of a very small number of well-to-do people in Ghana while everyone else has nothing? Can I keep quiet and mind my own business if I see injustice being done to someone else? Can I ignore poverty and ignorance when I can do something to improve the situation?

I may disagree with the government of the day. But I will not engage in acts that will disgrace my country and its people. I may not be a member of any ruling political party. But I have a duty to make contributions that will improve the quality of life of our people and the prosperity of our nation.

I have learned that Ghana is still a predominantly poor country. Some of us are lucky to be doing better than others are. But it is a short ride from well-to-do to poverty in this country. Therefore, I must lend my experience to the effort to improve the lot of the rural poor. I know to be careful to choose which initiatives to be associated with now that experience has shown that many rejoice in bringing people down. Success is still looking for a home in Ghana.

I am a CPP-ist. People wonder why an American-trained business professional can belong to the CPP family. But America teaches you that there is honor in fighting injustice of all types. America teaches you to value freedom. America welcomes the downtrodden and the persecuted masses from all over the world. Kwame Nkrumah experienced this. I believe Nkrumah's commitment to promoting the right of the poor, the downtrodden, to rise, be free, and gain the means to enjoy prosperity at home now gave birth to the CPP. Someday, when the CPP family awakens from its thirty-year slumber, I will be one of the faithful because we are not yet a prosperous nation.

I have become more Ghanaian. I am still on the journey back home. I remain positive about being here. And yes, whenever and wherever my opinion is sought, I will give it freely and without malice. I will travel abroad and live elsewhere from time to time, but this will forever remain my home.

Though it brought pain, sorrow, and grief, I am grateful for January 18, 1996. It is important to note that I went ahead to participate in the program at Wharton, where I was very well received. Then I went back home to face the situation that had developed.

My Thoughts on 1996 Speech
Delivered to the Rotary Club of Accra

December 11, 1995

I appreciate this opportunity to share with you my thoughts on 1996. Most importantly, I hope to encourage each and every one of you to choose to join the campaign for national team building and reconciliation. I hope all of you have read Mr. K. B. Asante's article in today's *Daily Graphic* newspaper. If you have not, please do so. The last paragraph of that article expresses many of my deep-felt sentiments in the most appropriate language.

There are many questions about 1996 and not enough answers. I will attempt to give you my perspective on what the situation is and what I believe needs to happen for us to avoid a serious collision in this country in 1996. First of all, we are on a collision course, and it will get worse if something significant is not done to reduce tension between political opponents.

We cannot afford the 1996 elections, yet the elections must go on. The cost to our society may be too high for us to bear. I have some reasons for this:

- As you all know, inflation is running at more than 70 percent and threatens to reach the 100 percent mark. Government borrowing is starving the private sector of the necessary opportunity to gain access to the investment capital. As a result, the private sector is not growing at the rate needed to make it the so-called engine of growth. Let me explain how serious this is. Several thousands of government workers have lost their jobs as a result of the economic recovery program. Many more workers from the civil service and state-owned enterprises will lose their jobs in 1996. The hope has been that retrenched workers would find employment in the private sector or start their own businesses. This will not happen because of the lack of easy access to and unavailability of capital. The 1996 elections will make this situation worse because government will spend more money on programs it feels will gain it more votes. The private sector will spend some of the little capital available to support parties of their choice. The picture, as you can see, could be a worsened economic situation.

- Then we have what I call "you kill me, I kill you" politics. It saddens me to say that I have come to realize that government and the opposition in Ghana really consider each other to be enemies. Many on both sides have sworn themselves to engage in a campaign of hate. Nothing good can come from the other side. The worst part about it is that much of the hatred stems from the existence of the dominant player on the political scene right now, J. J. Rawlings. I cannot explain this factor, and frankly, I do not even want to attempt to do so. All I know is that there is a fanatic display of "for" and "against" whenever the Rawlings factor comes in. Some people will do anything to keep Rawlings in power. Others will do anything to get him out of power. Neither side is right. But I fear that this also will not get better in 1996 because J. J. Rawlings is going to insist on serving the eight years the constitution allows a president to serve if he or she can win reelection. As someone has already written, if Rawlings wins in 1996, trouble; if he loses, trouble. The only way out is if he is not involved.

In 1996, global competition for investment, human capital, and markets will become more fierce. Ghana needs all the internal goodwill it needs in order to even stay its ground. To grow rapidly and become a developed nation, this country needs the talents of all of its men and women. But we are a nation wounded from the effects of self-appointed leaders and unjust punishment of citizens from 1966 to 1992. This country needs healing. The year 1996 is just around the corner, and our political leaders cannot even tolerate each other. How do we heal our wounds and have the hope that the best minds will be applied to our problems regardless of political, religious, and tribal affiliation when the current recognized political leaders cannot even agree to discuss our problems together? So I ask you again: Can we really afford the 1996 election?

Since we must have the 1996 elections, here are some perspectives, questions, and opinions:

- If the opposition really believes that only by getting together will they be able to defeat J. J. Rawlings, why do its leaders all want to be president? Why are they, the leaders themselves, not their appointees, not sitting together indoors to agree on some power-sharing formula? Are they all secretly hoping that they will become so popular that the other candidates will obviously recognize their superior strength and unite behind them? Is this greed, selfishness, or democracy?

- If the Alliance for Change (AFC), a civil society organization, really wants to be a unifying force for the opposition to win in 1996, why do they insist on being a catalyst? Why are they listening to the traditional parties? If they really want to make a direct impact, why aren't they getting themselves together as a major political party? Don't they know they have almost accomplished what Nkrumah did in the late 1950s and Rawlings did in 1992 by bringing together people from multiple political traditions?

- Why are the followers of Kwame Nkrumah finding it difficult to form one united front? Could it be that many of them are only using Nkrumah's name for selfish gain and do not really care for what he stood for? Would some of these so-called Nkrumaists not scatter if Nkrumah were to rise from the dead today?

- Why is the self-described people's democratic party, the NDC, the party with the self-described people's champion J. J. Rawlings, quickly acquiring the image of the money party? Why are some of its leaders determined to win the 1996 election by buying votes and not through logic? After being in charge during the "decade that ended the decay" and three years of dominance at the national, regional, and local levels under constitutional democracy, shouldn't the party's good works be enough to convince the voters that there is no challenger?

- Within the NDC, who comes after J. J. Rawlings? And I don't mean the other Dr. Rawlings. If the male Dr. Rawlings were all of a sudden to decide to do what a famous Ghanaian, Floyd Klutei Robertson, is supposed to have said and done on Ghanaian soil, sit in his corner and say "*menyaa*," what will the Akatamanso people do? Who is the fallback candidate? Can they hold together as a party? We know they will not go to Arkaah. So who is the successor? Is there a leadership crisis in the NDC?

I am only asking questions, remember? I am only here considering the fact that we have intelligent, smart, professional people, hardworking entrepreneurs, in this audience. I cannot pretend to know it all or have all the answers. I can only suggest that all of us look for answers to these questions, particularly on the matter of leadership.

At this point, I would like to ask for your support on the agenda to build a national team that brings healing to our people through a sincere program of national reconciliation. For want of a better term, I have called this idea "national government." All I am promoting is the use of the best talent available by the government of the day so we can achieve the best results possible.

Because of the current antagonistic nature of our winner-takes-all politics and our most recent past history of intolerance to opposition, we are not renewing our national leadership. Our potential leaders are frightened, starved of funds, intimidated by threats of physical violence, and denied of access to government contracts. Their ideas are seen as useless because they are inconsistent with the official message. We all agree that we need true peace and reconciliation to enable all elements of our country to work together. But it will require real statesmen and women to make that happen.

Imagine what will happen if J. J. Rawlings will go on national radio and television next month and declare that, if he wins in 1996, he will invite Adu-Boahen and anybody else who contests the presidential elections to nominate some of their best people to be part of a national team as ministers of state. Just think what will happen if J. J. Rawlings also says next month that he acknowledges the pain caused to some Ghanaians from 1966 to 1992. Therefore, he has authorized an independent commission chaired by someone like Bishop Sarpong or Rev. Dr. Dickson to review all cases presented and propose compensation to the extent feasible for implementation without revision.

What if the other presidential candidates made a similar commitment? Wouldn't that be wonderful? I can imagine what some of you are thinking. It is not possible. And isn't that a strong statement of the problem we have in this country? You and I do not have any choice but to persist in finding ways to make our situation better.

In conclusion, I wish to emphasize that we have abundant talent in this country, but it is parochial. The politics of exclusion is preventing our march forward. I have often said that African talent is the most bored talent in the world because it is looking for opportunity. It is starved of opportunity in Africa. We rejoice in attracting foreign investors from the United States, Malaysia, Germany, and elsewhere. We do not devote time and attention to encourage local investors. Some of us are where we are because we were given opportunity in other people's countries. But our own government is sometimes suspicious of us and prevents some of us from succeeding right here in our own country.

I do believe we will find a way to remove the barriers that prevent our government from encouraging more local private investors to succeed. We will find a way to encourage the government of the day to use the best talent we have, regardless of political, religious, and ethnic affiliation.

I believe that, with all of your active support and involvement, we will be able to forge a national team and bring about national reconciliation. Thank you for your kind attention.

I Stand Accused!

January 30, 1996

Without a doubt, I have learned more about my country Ghana and being Ghanaian in the country this past week than any other period in my life. I rode in the same plane with the minister of finance to Washington, DC, on Wednesday, January 17, 1996. We arrived in Washington, DC, on January 18. His mission, I assumed, was to review government's economic program and the proposed 1996 budget with the World Bank. My mission was to promote doing business in Ghana at the 22nd Annual Whitney Young Conference at the Wharton Business School in Philadelphia. Officials from the Ghana embassy welcomed the minister. He probably slept well that night. The immigration official welcomed me back home to the country I chose years ago as my country of permanent residence. In the car that took me to my house in Virginia, I was handed one of the many fax messages I had received from Ghana that day. I didn't sleep well that night.

On the front cover of the *Ghanaian Times* newspaper on January 18 was a story about a Serious Fraud Office investigation on the activities and contracts awarded by the State Enterprises Commission. In the middle of the story was a feature about me and alleged dubious business transactions I was alleged to have engaged in. I knew the story was inaccurate. But I also knew the people who actually wrote the story carefully made sure that

17

the inaccuracies were given prominence. Would the editor of the *Ghanaian Times* write such a story or the accompanying editorial about me himself without any attempt to ascertain accuracy from me? Would a professional journalist write those two pieces? Would a newspaper treat a features contributor so shabbily? I had written articles for this newspaper that had been published. So they knew how to find me if they wanted to. The story and editorial were obviously written and sent to the newspaper from somewhere else. I knew then that I had finally arrived on the Ghanaian social and political scene.

The colonial authorities who tried to hang on to the power of government accused Kwame Nkrumah of all sorts of economic sabotage and subversive activities. He actually did serve time in prison. Nelson Mandela's troubles with the South African authorities under apartheid are now legendary. So I was not the only one that politics in Africa had thrown dirt at. Was I accused of plotting a coup against government? Had I attempted to break into a bank? Had I committed murder? Had I stolen money from anyone? No!

What is worse is that, after hauling me before the Serious Fraud Office (SFO) and making a public show of it all, the whole investigation was stopped. No more invitations for interviews by the SFO, no invitation by the attorney general's office, and no official report by the SFO to deal with. I would later learn what a senior advisor to the Rawlings administration meant. "They were disappointed that I had turned out not to be on their side contrary to their expectations." Another Ghanaian political appointee in Washington, DC, looked at my wife and me and told us to our face, "They had to squeeze you for being too known." All of this was to make sure that I could not threaten their political fortunes in Ghana.

For the benefit of my fellow Ghanaians, I have attempted to chronicle my wrongdoings:

- **Charge Number 1:** I decided to make my life more interesting and valuable to my birth country. I wasn't satisfied with the life of a Big Six public accounting firm partner in Washington, DC. Earning a very good income with a house in suburban Washington, DC, a

Mercedes-Benz and Volvo in the driveway, and so forth were not enough. I needed more spice in my life and, in the process, wanted to help my country to develop. I went against the advice of my partners and chose to persist in ensuring that our international firm set up a world-class consulting firm in West Africa. I am thankful that I heeded part of their advice and did not move immediately to establish permanent residence in West Africa. I am also thankful that I did not sever my ties with the international firm. I count myself lucky that the consulting firm was set up for all of West Africa and not just Ghana. But I made sure that Ghana became the administrative headquarters for the firm.

- **Charge Number 2:** I made the mistake of asking government officials I met when I started my frequent trips in and out of Ghana if there were anything I could do to help. That landed our international firm unpaid assignments from the private and public sectors, including the Ashanti Goldfields Company and the Ministry of Finance and Economic Planning. We also earned additional consulting engagements to be paid for. Three of the engagements we performed for the public sector are yet to be paid for. I personally worked on those assignments as if they were for my own personal enterprises. In the process, some confused our diligent and persistent manner of implementing government policy with us being on government payroll. The mother of all sins is that our firm insisted on being paid international rates comparable to what other international consultants earn on the same or similar engagements. To compound that sin, here was a Ghanaian as dark skinned as any other earning the top dollar only reserved for foreigners.

- **Charge Number 3:** I decided to buy a house in Ghana in 1994 so that, while I worked, my children could live here and perhaps get to know and like their father's country. Hopefully, they would also have Ghanaian classmates for future's sake. I bought a house in highly visible North Ridge. I am sorry. I didn't know that such hideous acts were to be committed at East Legon and beyond.

I blame all my so-called friends who have been living in Ghana all these years for not giving me proper advice as soon as I stepped foot at the Accra Airport. But then, how could they have known that I would turn out to be so troublesome? It is not their fault.

- **Charge Number 4:** I decided to invest serious money in my own country. I engaged in my own private economic recovery program by working together with my wife to build a resort and conference center in my hometown, Elmina. We created full-time jobs for more than fifty people in 1993 by this action. Never mind that my wife and I owe some banks as a result. Never mind that we have reinvested every pesewa this facility has earned to expand it and add more attractive features. Never mind that now the District Assembly, the IRS, SSNIT, and various suppliers earn revenues from our investment. I am told that, even before the resort received its first guest, rumors were already circulating in Accra that I was building a Ghana Camp David! I have often wondered why General Acheampong tried (but failed) to outlaw rumormongering.

- **Charge Number 5:** Many have told me that my most serious charge is that I could become a J. J. Rawlings challenger. I have been asked, "Who are you to discuss the pros and cons of the Rawlings presidency?" Why would I have the nerve to consider that a multiparty national government made up of the best Ghanaian talent available could lead to breakthrough social and economic results for the country? I even said this on TV and radio! Didn't all those people who invited me to be on radio and TV programs know I had a mind with views and a sufficiently "okro mouth" to match?

Let's get one thing straight. I am an Nkrumaist. I share the late super president's vision of building a strong, prosperous, proud Ghana now while I am still alive. This fact is not a crime. Who I vote for in the 1996 election is my private, constitutional right. I am not seeking to become president of this country in 1996. Those who are eager to serve in that office should devote their energies to sell their good deeds and their vision for the country to the voters. That will be a more fruitful activity to engage in.

So fellow Ghanaians, "How for do?" Call me ambitious. Call me naïve. Tell me I don't know Ghana. Okay, fault me for engaging in so many business activities. I want to live a good life, and I don't mind working hard for it. Consider me irreverent sometimes. But serious fraud? Wallahi! Someone miss road badly!

Letter to the Editor of
the *Ghanaian Times*

February 7, 1996
The Editor of the *Ghanaian Times*, Accra
Dear Sir:

Ghanaian Times News Story on Serious Fraud Investigation

I returned from my recent trip to the United States of America to participate in a workshop on business opportunities in Ghana at the Wharton Business School and to promote business opportunities in Ghana on Wednesday, January 24, 1996. The *Ghanaian Times* story of January 18 reported allegations that I was the target of a Serious Fraud Office investigation.

Since the story was published, all government (central government and state-owned enterprises) contracts with Deloitte & Touche Consulting have been canceled. The livelihood of several law-abiding and taxpaying Ghanaians who are employees of the firm has been seriously threatened. No formal reasons have been given for these actions. Informally, the officials involved cite "orders from above" due to the *Ghanaian Times* story and the serious fraud investigations.

I have also been removed from the board of directors of the Ghana Airways Company Limited without cause and without reason. Who is hiding behind the story and why? Who orchestrated these acts? Life will go on. Truth will prevail. Those who seek to destroy will, in this case, surely not succeed. God, we all know, acts in mysterious ways. What we know for sure is that He always protects the innocent.

I have consulted my lawyer. He is taking appropriate steps to ascertain the legal implications of the actions taken by the various arms of government and the *Ghanaian Times*. My lawyer and I have sought confirmation from the Serious Fraud Office on whether or not I am a specific target of their alleged investigations. They are quite firm that I am not a target of their investigations. They also state strongly that they are not the source of the story published in the *Ghanaian Times*.

It seems to me then that the story was an organized attempt by faceless and nameless people to deliberately damage the international personal and professional reputation I have built at great cost and effort. It also seems to me that the story was also an effort organized to damage the reputation and financial standing of the international public accounting and management consulting firm that I represent in Africa.

I do not have a problem with government taking back its appointments or contracts. I do have a problem with wrongful accusation of serious fraud. I also do have a problem with using information from an incomplete investigation to form judgments publicly.

It is important that the real truth in this matter is determined through proper legal channels. I intend to fully cooperate with properly constituted authorities in their investigations. I am also determined that the public will know the whole truth when the alleged investigations are concluded. I have informed the Serious Fraud Office of my readiness to meet and discuss my contracts with the State Enterprises Commission with them.

In the meantime, I entreat all members of the press to exercise circumspection in relation to what they write about these alleged investigations. I also wish to state for the record that I sent a rejoinder on the story to the *Ghanaian Times* over two weeks ago. The fact you have not seen it fit to publish is disturbing to me. While I am aware of the *Ghanaian Times* constitutional obligation to publish the rejoinder, I am more concerned about the effect unresearched stories alleging fraud can do to the ability of our fragile economy to attract qualified Ghanaians abroad to return to this country. I am also concerned about its effect on potential international investors.

Already, I have heard from my colleagues in the United Kingdom and North America about the serious fraud allegations. They heard the news through international communications channels such as the Internet. What may seem like a little, harmless local story has been heard and read across the ocean. It has resulted in unnecessary negative economic consequences.

Our country needs the goodwill of all of its people to succeed where many other African countries have failed economically, politically, and socially. We must encourage everyone to succeed. We must look to reward success and not to destroy it.

We must do everything possible—but positively—to make sure that Ghanaians do the right things. We must have visible positive role models. And we must believe in what is good about our fellow Ghanaians. When that happens, we will enjoy prosperity, and the much sought-after foreign investor will also feel comfortable with us.

Very truly yours,
P. Kwesi Nduom, PhD, CMC

Suggestions to Protect the National Interest in 1996

February 24, 1996

I have had several discussions with numerous Ghanaians over what can be called "the national interest." Many agree that the national interest concerns all of us. Everyone agrees that the national interest can be served equally and just as well by the people in the private sector and not just those in the public sector. Businesspeople, politicians, teachers, journalists, engineers, soldiers, the rich, the poor, and so forth all have a duty to protect the national interest.

No one group, body, or individual has the sole responsibility of seeking and protecting the national interest. At various times in our history as a nation, some segment of our population has sought to monopolize the national interest. Others have left the national interest to the few who find themselves in government.

But what is this so-called national interest? It is what all citizens of a country have in common. It is what we share in common. And it defines our being as citizens of a country and gives us inalienable rights to freedom, property, fair trial, security, prosperity, and so forth. It gives us the right to join political, social, or religious groups of our choice. We share the state of the economy, the strength of the currency, the security of our national geographic borders, and the efficiency of institutions like the police, judiciary, military, and public schools. In this regard, it is a wonder that we sometimes think or behave as if we are really independent of each other. When we do something against someone's individual freedom or civil right, we take something from ourselves because we all share a common national interest.

Sometimes, we assume only those in government or the political party in power has the responsibility to protect the national interest. Government officials themselves sometimes make the mistake by thinking the national interest starts and ends with them. Those in the military often invoke the national interest when they overthrow civilian or military governments. Security agents sometimes conduct investigations or initiate acts against individual citizens under the context or pretext of protecting that part of the national interest called security. Thus, while the national interest is for all of us to protect, it is the very reason often given for denying citizens one basic right, freedom.

It is 1996. An election year. A critical election year. This election year will tell Ghanaians and the rest of the world that we are ready to allow one civilian government to succeed another through the ballot box for the first time in thirty years. Whichever political party wins the presidency in 1996, Ghana will be able to stake its claim as a democratic state. I am convinced that a healthy dose of concern and action to protect our collective national interest will make this significant election year peaceful and successful. I have a few suggestions to make:

- **To business leaders:** You can protect the national interest by helping the private sector grow strong and powerful to neutralize the stranglehold government has on the economy and, through it, the lives of Ghanaians. It is tempting to decide not to invest in an election year. It is very tempting to change your cedis to dollars and pounds and bank them outside the country as insurance against possible attacks by government agencies. Think about it. Without your continuous investment, who will create jobs? Who will create the wealth needed for our economy to grow? Unemployment and poverty threaten the national interest. Those in the private sector can provide the long-term security the economy needs.

- **To politicians:** If one group is confused about its role in protecting the national interest, it is politicians. Those in government tend to use "national interest" to punish citizens they see as their opponents. Those in opposition tend to use the same "national interest" to oppose the plans and actions of government. Some politicians in government forget they wield power so significant that their actions can shatter the lives of individuals and, with it, dilute our national interest. Government officials can prosecute, jail, execute, refuse licenses, impose penalties, deny permits, and so forth. Politicians in 1996 should think kind and act gently. I am sure that, for politicians who will end up in government, it will be important to have an opposition group that is willing to cooperate with you so you can really govern in the national interest without worrying about your self-interest all the time. Instead of search-and-destroy tactics, the opposition should use a positive approach by publicizing the alternatives they have to offer. Opposition politicians aim to inherit a governable country. Their actions and conduct must not lead to the tearing of things down so badly that, should they win, they will spend most of their time blaming the former government for leaving a difficult situation instead of implementing new programs.

- **To journalists:** Journalists from both the state and private media houses should know the tremendous influence they carry in the country. Many of you know that, even if you have to retract a story, apologize, or pay a fine, you would have already damaged the reputation of someone or caused injury of some type. What does it benefit the country if you leave the impression that all businesspeople are crooks and thieves? Does it benefit the country if you leave the impression that all government officials are corrupt? By all means, the press must investigate injustice and allegations of corruption and bring out all the news the public has a right to be informed about. In this country, many readers have chosen to ignore or consider everything written or broadcast by the state media to be false. What national interest can be served by the state media if it has very little or no credibility with the public? On the other hand, some in the private media consider themselves on a crusade against government or specific government officials. For them, the only news fit to print is what can hurt, injure, and discredit. It is possible then to not only hurt government but the national interest we are all concerned about. But we can all agree that a balanced press can indeed protect the freedom of expression interest that is so fundamental to ensuring the protection of other critical elements of our national interest.

- **To the general public:** Many of you consider your interests secure if you can eat, get paid at the end of the month, have a job, and get a place to sleep. For some of you, journalists are troublesome. Many of you think that politics is a crooked game to be played by crooked people. So why do you complain when government ignores your needs or does the wrong thing? Perhaps some of you should think about the "garbage in, garbage out" theory computer people are taught religiously. What national interest is served when you decide to look on unconcerned or even blame the victim for inviting trouble when someone is unjustly accused or harassed? Does the fact that sometimes you just want to mind your own business not prove that we have many issues we all (not just government people) have to resolve? If you believe, as many of you do, that our society has become more intolerant, mediocre, and less successful economically than you expect, shouldn't you try to do something about it?

We all have a role to play to make things better. The national interest requires us all to be more concerned, more inquisitive, more tolerant, and more willing to find solutions to national problems. The more positive ways we find to show concern, the more positive solutions we will find. I am confident that we will find a way to protect our collective national interest in 1996. After all, what other country is there for us?

Constraints to Investing In Ghana "Independence Means Not Having to Beg Your Neighbor for a Cigarette Tin of Gari" Presented at the Continuing Legal Education Programme Workshop of the Ghana Bar Association

March 11, 1996

Introduction

First of all, I would like to express my appreciation to the Ghana Bar Association for the invitation to discuss a few thoughts about constraints to investing in Ghana. I must congratulate your association for its active participation and the tremendous positive contribution it has made to the cause of human rights, freedom of speech, and democracy in this country. I am first and foremost an economic animal. Therefore, as an investment advisor, I hope the members of your reputable association will also take an active interest in promoting the cause of local investors so we can all help make our nation a prosperous one.

I have taken note of the fact that the theme for your workshop is the "Legal Environment for Investment in Ghana." I cannot pretend to have much technical knowledge about legal matters. As a matter of fact, I try as much as possible to avoid the law, especially its punitive effects. As a prudent person, I try to seek legal advice whenever and wherever there is the possibility of facing legal action of any type, positive or negative.

Here am I, a risk-averse person as far as legal matters go, standing in the company of a frightening collection of brilliant, legal talent. So I wish to avoid conflict with the law and legal minds by staying as far away as possible from the technicalities of investment law and how they affect investment in Ghana. But that is not to say that I plan to sidestep the topic. Today, I would not even like to talk from my usual perspective of a detached professional management consultant or investment advisor but from the practical perspective of an entrepreneur. That way, you can be sure that what I tell you is based on fact or the truth. If I happen to misinterpret the truth slightly, but just slightly, I beg you in advance not to file a suit against me to prevent me from further public speaking. I wouldn't want anyone cause any court to enjoin some potentially unfriendly third party to my case.

I should let you know that a couple people called me when they saw my name in your announcement about this workshop as a speaker. They were alarmed that I the person currently in trouble with the authorities would want to spoil my case further by associating with the troublesome GBA people. I stand here to tell you that such comments do not bother me. I feel proud to be in your company.

I, like many in our society today, have had the privilege of having studied and worked abroad. In my case, I happen to have ended up in the United States of America. As a result of this experience, I have come to expect something more from my own country of origin. I know a little bit about the difficulties this country has gone through over the past fifteen years and indeed over the past thirty-nine years of independence. It is indeed good and a marvel that we have been able to accomplish what we all see around us in Ghana.

But permit me to be ungrateful, greedy, and impatient. I am not impressed by what we collectively have been able to accomplish as a nation after thirty-nine years of independence. We can do better than being an officially sanctioned and internationally recognized nation of beggars. We can do more. We can do a lot more in a very short period of time if we pay concentrated and tunnel vision–type attention to the subjects of economics and investment and pay less attention to politics.

If anyone is so enamored of the 1996 political fever that they take political offense at anything I say, that would be unfortunate because I do not see a country of NDC, NPP, or CPP people. I see Ghanaians. My intent here today is not political. I want to live very well in a Ghana that is a prosperous country. I hope you all want to do the same. I don't want to wait until I am seventy years old to realize that a dream has passed me by. I speak only as an intensely interested Ghanaian.

Investors have to deal with a few key but practical questions before they decide to invest in any country. To place the discussion of constraints to investing in Ghana in the proper perspective, I will attempt to describe what I consider to be enabling conditions for investment. I will describe all of them briefly, and then I will go back and discuss the situation pertaining to each one of them in Ghana.

Enabling Ingredients for Investments

The ingredients I consider to be key enablers for investments are institutional and legal framework, local talent, social and political environment, and attitude toward private sector investment.

Legal Framework

Some business classes teach students to distinguish between risk lovers and those who are risk averse. The impression is created that entrepreneurs are risk lovers. Some think, to win big in business, you have to take big risks. Investors or entrepreneurs do not take risks. They are not risk takers, but rather, they are risk managers. They do not like risky situations. An investor will assess a situation and determine if there is a charted or uncharted course to be followed for economic advantage.

An investor will not invest his capital where the law prevents it. The investor does not want to invest if the law prevents him from earning a profit. The investor also wants to invest where the law makes it possible to cash in the investment and profits earned and, if need be, move the money somewhere else in a timely manner. The foreign investor, in particular, wants to invest where his investment and profits can be converted easily into the foreign currency of choice.

An investor will want to know if profits earned will be heavily taxed or not because he wants to earn the maximum return possible. This expectation applies whether we are talking about direct or indirect investment. Direct investment is where Kwaku takes his 10 million cedis to the Afram Plains to construct and manage a factory to produce rice beer. Indirect investment is where Abena takes her 10 million cedis to Gold Coast Securities to buy Ghana Commercial Bank shares.

A lot of this institutional and legal framework for investing can be found in a country's investment code, tax laws, and company registration laws. By institutional framework, I mean, for example, those institutions or offices that have the responsibility for controlling investment activity such as the Bank of Ghana, Ghana Stock Exchange, and Office of the Registrar-General.

Local Talent

Local talent is a critical ingredient not mentioned much but one that is very essential to the success of investments. Astute investors, particularly those with a choice of where to invest, search hard to find well-trained local labor. Local talent with good work ethic can be a very strong, positive magnet for investments. You will find that countries like Japan, Korea, Singapore, Ireland, and Germany with rapid post–World War II economic growth have developed excellent local universities and technical institutions. Their people are relatively well paid at home. You do not hear those countries complaining of brain drain.

Social and Political Environment

Any talk about investments has to deal with the element of political and social environment. I have learned that this tends to be a controversial issue in Ghana. But it needs not be. Political and social stability is an important enabler for both local and foreign investors. It does not take a genius or astute analyst to take stock of the political and social situations in West Africa and the rest of Africa both south and north of the Sahara. Religious, ethnic, and political conflicts abound. Civil wars, genocide, military coups, and gross public financial mismanagement have defined our environment.

The political and social environment in West Africa in general over the past six months has not been a welcoming one for investments. Gambia has a military government that is trying against significant international odds to hold the country together. Many former civilian government officials there have been barred from traveling outside their villages. In Sierra Leone, there is hunger and the threat of rebel attacks that make even ordinary living difficult. There is uneasy calm in Côte d'Ivoire after their recent elections. In that country, two journalists have been jailed for writing that the president's bad luck caused the local football club ASEC to lose a championship match to a South African team. In Niger, a military coup caused international aid agencies to suspend badly needed aid to that country.

Just a few weeks ago, if you were in Conakry, you would have witnessed not only a military assault on the presidential palace, but the frightening destruction of business assets. If you had $10 million to invest and you had your choice of countries to invest it in, would you choose Guinea?

Attitude toward Private Sector Investments

A country's collective attitude toward private sector investments can be a significant enabler or an invisible, yet solid, barrier to investments. I refer to a collective attitude because it pertains to both the citizens of a country and the government. If government or the citizens of a country believe that only the state should invest and take profit, the private sector will suffer. If government or the citizens believe there is something illegal or unacceptable about private sector investment, the country will frown upon private sector wealth and success. Investors do not like to risk their capital in such an environment.

Constraints to Investments in Ghana

I will now take each one of these enablers and examine them to determine if they represent constraints to investments in Ghana.

Legal Framework

An important document on Ghana's investment legal framework is the Ghana Investment Promotion Centre Act, 1994 (ACT478). Technically, it is difficult to find significant flaws in the document that any serious investor local or foreign can argue about. Compared to other similar investment acts worldwide, it sets a good framework within which we can promote investments in Ghana. Similarly, our tax laws, comparatively speaking, do not present a constraint to investments. The recent move to repeal the stamp duty on the sale of stocks to foreigners is a progressive one. Its passage into law by Parliament will make the legal framework for investing in Ghana more attractive to foreigners.

So you may ask: Are there any constraints to investing in Ghana presented by the legal and institutional framework? The constraints presented by the institutional and legal framework are not due to technical or policy matters. They are constraints imposed by the flawed implementation of the legal framework and matters we can only ascribe to the "human factor" or "human error."

I have found that many of those charged with implementation often discriminate in favor of government-affiliated institutional investors and foreign investors to the detriment of local, private entrepreneurs.

Some create their own unwritten laws to frustrate the efforts of the local investor.

One example in the area of implementation is the multiple roles the governor of the Bank of Ghana plays with financial institutions:

- The governor is the government's key fiscal policy advisor. The central bank plays a very important role in monitoring and indeed regulating the supply of money in the country.
- The governor not only licenses and regulates bank, he plays the same role for nonbank financial institutions as well.
- The governor is the sole regulatory commissioner over the capital markets and the activities of brokerage houses in the country. I am not here to suggest that the current governor is deficient in his duties. However, the fact that one person has been saddled with all these huge and significant responsibilities presents a potentially enormous damaging constraint on investing in Ghana. There are not enough hours in a day to allow one person or institution to play all these roles in a timely, effective manner. And we all know that time is money when it comes to financial matters.

When nonbank financial institutions, the Ghana Stock Exchange with its brokerage houses, and other capital markets innovations dawned on Ghana, the prudent thing to do would have been to ensure the constitution of the relevant regulatory agencies with their requisite policies, procedures, and personnel in the shortest possible time.

In the capital markets, transparency in getting licenses to do business approved, getting transactions authorized to go to market, and disciplining institutional players are of paramount concern.

There is reason to believe that this much-needed transparency is currently not established. Some do indeed obtain licenses to operate banks, nonbank financial institutions, funds, and other financial institutions. But others have had to wait months and years for no apparent official reasons. Investment capital is nonpatient capital.

Abundant Local Talent

It is my clear and unequivocal opinion that there is abundant local talent in this country to support any type of investment. But we do have at least two troublesome issues to address in this area:

- The first has to do with the difficulties we face in financing secondary and university education. There is the related problem brought about by the interruption in producing graduates as a result of the closure of universities. I see this as an issue perhaps not immediately facing the investor but one that will become quite apparent in the next two to five years.
- The second and more immediate issue has to do with how to compensate talented local professionals (and, for that matter, all grades of workers).

Since I have been associated with a certain probe by a certain agency with a seriously threatening name, I cannot discuss the specific merits or demerits of that situation. However, consider that, in this country, some people consider it illegal for a Ghanaian citizen to earn foreign currency. They claim foreigners can earn foreign currency in Ghana but not Ghanaian citizens.

Is it true or false that, in this country, there are consultants working for all arms, or is it bodies of government who earn anywhere from 500 to 3,000 British pounds a day? Are these Ghanaians or foreigners? If they are foreigners and their Ghanaian counterparts can only earn about 100,000 cedis a day, what message are we trying to give to talented Ghanaian professionals? Clearly, we are saying that, if you are good and Ghanaian and if you want to earn good money, leave the country! If our talented professionals leave, who will be here to support the investor? Perhaps as some companies have already done, they will turn around and bring in expatriate professionals. They will pay them high expatriate salaries transferred to overseas accounts because we do not have people with the requisite experience and expertise here. Even more important, how do we expect the Ghanaian to have the money to invest in Ghana when we are only prepared to pay low professional fees and salaries? Enough said.

Political and Social Environment

As I said earlier, this always tends to be a controversial subject. All Ghanaians have a right to feel proud about the fact that the opposition groups, government, the military, the press (both private and state-owned), the labor unions, the bar association, and others have all collaborated very well to create a level of stability that stands apart clearly as a positive island to the chaos that surrounds us in West Africa. Compared to many West African countries, we have a relatively desirable political and social stability. In a way, this is most unfortunate because you want to compare yourself with the best. You want to soar with the eagles, roar with the lions, and not play games with mice. In reality, potential foreign investors looking at Africa in general most of the time talk about Ghana, South Africa, Botswana, Morocco, and, if they are French, Côte d'Ivoire. Ghana is an "in" country in West Africa thanks to the levelheadedness of our people.

In my view, the only constraint to investing in Ghana in this area is a potential one, the 1996 elections. Some potential investors are awaiting the elections because they fear a violent outcome if the results are disputed. There is cause for concern since some in our society seem prepared to put their quest for political power above the social and economic stability of the nation. Some are behaving as if this country belongs to them and only they can be president, ministers, and members of Parliament. Believe me, this attitude can constitute a serious constraint to investing in Ghana.

Attitude toward the Private Sector

It is my considered opinion that it is in this area that we have the greatest constraint to investment in Ghana. This constraint comes from both government or official channels and individual Ghanaians.

We have come from a history in this country of state dominance over investment and employment. The state remains a dominant player in many sectors of the economy. For many, their attitude toward the private sector started in secondary school when the excellent students were encouraged to become science students, the okay ones were arts students, and the rest were business or commerce students. One military regime in this country equated business with "*kalabule* (profiteering)." In another regime, a high bank account was grounds for investigation. To some, poverty is to be celebrated. To them, wealth is to be scorned. It belongs to the state. If you have it, you must have stolen it. How can someone succeed where he doesn't know even how to begin to try? This attitude encourages the practice of mediocrity where entrepreneurs only do just enough to satisfy their own needs and wants because to invest big and win big and make big money attracts envy and public suspicion.

Many private investors bought Social Security Bank shares because it was a state bank. The proceeds went to the state. It was fine with them. Not too long ago, some refused to buy Mechanical Lloyd shares. Why, they asked, should they give that private family more money? Again, the same group of individual investors and, this time, institutional investors refused to buy Top Industries shares. Why give money to those private individuals? Those same investors are getting ready to buy Ghana Commercial Bank shares. Giving to the state is good; giving to the private sector is bad.

And yet, the Rawlings-led administration says the private sector should be the engine of economic growth in this economy. What magic are we waiting for? In my view, the negative attitude to private investment represents our most serious constraint to investing in Ghana.

Conclusion

I have tried to stay away from legal technicalities of investing in Ghana. I have attempted to use a practical approach to describe the key constraints to investments in Ghana. I have identified them as:

- Human errors associated with the implementation of the legal framework to making investments in Ghana
- Our reluctance to pay local talent the adequate compensation that can help fuel local investment
- Threats to our relatively stable political and social environment due to the impending general elections
- The lingering negative attitude toward private sector investments and wealth

Thank you for giving me the opportunity to share my thoughts on this important subject with you.

Speech Delivered at the 66th Speech and Prize-Giving Day of St. Augustine's College

March 23, 1996

I wish to thank the headmaster of St. Augustine's, the staff, and the board of governors for the great honor they have done to me by inviting me to be the guest speaker on the occasion of this year's speech and prize-giving event. I feel especially honored because, only twenty-five years ago, I myself sat here as a student on this same campus to listen to what I then thought to be some boring speech.

I must commend the headmaster and his staff and the students because I have been coming to this school consistently over the past five years, but this year, the campus looks much cleaner and brighter. I do hope this has also translated into academic enthusiasm and excellent performance in many areas.

Today, I propose to engage in a heart-to-heart conversation with the students gathered here. After all, this is their day. The rest of us are mere spectators, even though the parents and guardians here who have invested so much in the students are more than interested supporters. So I ask you, the students, to give me your attention for just a few minutes. I want to acknowledge today, as I do every day, that I am a lucky man. I am lucky to be from the wonderful territory called Elmina. I am lucky to have excellent parents who have served as a source of encouragement. I am lucky to have the best wife and supporter anyone can even dream of having. But today, I want you to know that I feel very lucky that I had the opportunity to be a student at St. Augustine's. I don't want this to be a one-way speech. I also don't want you to think as I thought a few years ago that this is some boring speech. So since this is a Christian institution, I want you to help me by giving me some Christian responses. If you feel proud to be an Augustinian, shout "Amen!" Thank you.

I want to ask the students here a simple question: Do you know how talented you are? Please help me and turn to the person next to you. Ask him or her: Do you know how talented you are? If you believe you have talent, say "Amen!"

Do you know what talent is? It is something special that all of you have. But don't get me wrong. Talent is not skill or the knowledge you gain by studying from midnight to daylight. It is not the *apo* (inside information) you gain from your teachers for your examinations. You know, when you go to the intercollege athletics events, some of you practice the lines you are going to lay on the first beautiful girl you meet very hard. Some have sleepless nights memorizing the lines. You press your clothes until it looks really tough. But when you get there, much as you have practiced it, the lines just don't flow. And the girls don't come. But some rascal just throws on any rags he can find. He sleeps soundly at night and doesn't even think about lines. He goes, and the lines just start flowing like seawater. And he has babes hanging all over him. He has talent. Praise talent! Amen!

Talent is God-given. Man cannot add or take anything from it. Sometimes we Africans or black people think we have problems because God gave us bad talent and gave the white people good talent. I am sure you have heard some of the old sayings, "Bronyi ara nye John." Even in the area of witchcraft, those who believe in it want us to believe that white people use their witchcraft to do good things, like go to the moon. We Africans, they say, use our witchcraft to steal, kill, and hurt others.

Don't believe it! God doesn't create garbage. He made all of us in His own image. If we believe that God loves all His children equally, then we must believe that He gave His black and white children equal doses of talent to do well. So turn to the person sitting next to you. Tell him or her, "God gave you good talent." Amen!

Your talent is equal to that of any European or American. If you go to many major corporations in the United States, you will find people like you and me. Many as dark skinned as I am performing with distinction in the white man's own country. They are in big, responsible positions because they use their talent well. If you go to General Motors, AT&T, IBM, the World Bank, and other international organizations, you will know what I am talking about. If you go to Washington, DC, one of my classmates from St. Augustine's is a very successful medical doctor with his own office. He lives in a very big mansion with a swimming pool and a nice, expensive car. He has many, many patients, black and white, who trust his wonderful African talent. But he is not unique. If you go to one of the world's biggest investment bankers in the world, you will also find one of my classmates making millions of dollars of revenues for the company. Another one of our classmates at St. Augustine's played with the Chicago Symphony Orchestra. Right here in Ghana, we have a classmate who is a minister of state. How could I myself, a regular boy from Elmina, go to this big United States and become one of four black partners out of two thousand partners in an international public accounting and consulting company? The main reason can only be God-given talent. All of you have it. Recognize it, and pursue it with all your strength. If you want to use your talent, say "Amen!"

But you may ask: If we Africans have this wonderful gift from God, why are our countries so poor? Why are many of the success stories involving even my own classmates not occurring in Africa but in North America and Europe? The answers come easily. Many Africans are not choosing to recognize and use their talent. We fail to prepare ourselves to take advantage of opportunities that come in life. We see opportunities as problems. If we have talent given by God, then we have the responsibility to exercise it to its fullest extent. In life, people become mediocre, envious, and jealous of what others are able to achieve because they do not try hard enough to discover what their own specific talent is. Some who know their gift do not pursue it with hard work and persistence.

The problem in Africa is our environment, which does not encourage a strong work ethic and success. A big part of this poor environment is our leaders. Many of them see success only in grabbing power and lording it over others. You have it here in your school as well. You know your good prefects and the bad ones. The good ones encourage others to succeed. When they see success, they point to it and ask others to emulate the good example. They lead by example. They do not order people around. They do not insist that only they should wear good clothes and eat the best foods. Indeed, your good leaders serve. You know the bad ones. They have no good ideas of their own. If you come up with good ideas, they will shout you down but turn around and make the ideas their own. Since they did not think of it, they make a mess of implementing it. They use physical violence to show they have power. Tell me. Am I wrong?

Not using your talent breeds mediocrity. Mediocrity breeds envy. Envy drives mediocre people to try to destroy what others have used their God-given talent to build. I beg you to help eliminate this disease in our African society. Start discovering your talent now. Start appreciating the success of others now. If you do, you will go very far in life yourself.

We are not all talented in the same way. That causes me to ask: Do you know how good you are? And do you know how good you can be? There is a well-known surgeon in a hospital in Ghana who I am told found it very difficult to pass the former Standard Seven or middle school examinations. He could not write one good sentence without a spelling or grammatical error or "bullet."

The story is that, during one exam, when the other students were sweating and writing pages, he was looking around the room, wondering what the heat was all about. The essay question was: Was the war between the Fantis and Ashantis inevitable? Discuss. His answer was yes. Finished. They thought he was stupid. But he just couldn't handle English and history. They bored him.

If you just give him physics, math, and a frog to dissect, he was in heaven. Luckily for him, he discovered his talent early enough to keep persisting until he passed Standard Seven and went to secondary school as a mature student. His patients now thank God he is a surgeon.

Do you know how good you are? What is your God-given talent? Have you thought about it? Many of our classmates tried hard to become science students because it was felt that the bright students went on to become medical doctors, engineers, and architects. Arts students were barely tolerated. Business or commerce students were at the bottom of the honor list. Many students with wonderful talent in music, painting, and languages forced themselves to become scientists. They were not gifted to be scientists. As a result, they did not pursue the science careers with enthusiasm. Many of them today are struggling with their lives because they were not encouraged to develop their God-given talent in arts and business.

Do you know how good you can be? When I was in Form One, a terrible thing happened after the first term exams. We came back to school to find that the three Form One classrooms had been reorganized according to how we did on our first term exams.

The students who placed in the first thirty positions on the exams were located in Form One A. The second thirty or so were in Form One B. The last thirty or so students were thrown into the exciting class called Form One C. Form One A was boring. During night studies, not even the famous Augustine's mosquitoes could entice them to look away from their physics and math books. Form One B was okay. But Form One C was fun. Every night was a disco or a world heavyweight boxing championship fight. Those not singing or boxing were writing love letters to Holy Child or *mons* students. I ask you: Did the Form One C students know how good they were? But equally important, did the Form One A students know how good they could be? One Form C student is now an assistant vice president of the internationally known Citibank in New York. He has a master's degree in business administration. He just played a leading role in the opening of a Citibank branch in Tanzania. Praise the Lord! Can you say "Amen" to that? He did it in spite of an environment that said, "You are not good enough; therefore, you will be placed among others who are equally not good enough." He found his talent. He persisted in wanting to succeed. He has found out how good he is. I ask you: Do you know how good you are? And do you know how good you can be?

Why am I weighing you down with all this talent talk? The Ghana government in the past five years has dismissed (they call it redeployment) more than one hundred thousand workers. IBM, the computer giant in the United States; Boeing, the company that manufactures airplanes; big insurance companies in North America; Ford Motors; and others have dismissed together more than one million workers in the past three years! Some hospitals in the United States are sending the medical doctors home. Top executives are being sent home. Not because they have stolen anything, but because their skills are no longer needed and companies are cutting cost. This world has become a more difficult and complex place. Over the next two years, the sale of state-owned enterprises will cause at least ten thousand employees to lose their jobs. All of you hope to become employed in Ghana or in another country in this world. As has been written on one tro-tro (minibus), "Nowhere Cool." Only the ones who choose to constantly exercise their talent and learn new skills will succeed. Are you using your time here profitably to discover your real talent? Are you learning to be better African leaders than those who have landed us in a position of disadvantage today? Do you know how good you are?

All of you have wonderful, positive God-given talent. Find out what specific talent God gave you. Be proud of it, and develop it. Use it to your advantage. You will not know how good you are if you do not take advantage of any opportunities given to make use of your talent. Do not envy those who are successful. Find out how they do well, and learn from them.

Find your own corner in the world, and be encouraged to persevere in your area of interest. Work hard at the things you like, and take advantage of any opportunities that come your way. Be ready, and be prepared. Luck helps. But the lucky ones are those who have prepared themselves and recognize their talent ahead of luck.

Not too long ago, I was one of you. I played in a band, and I played on the school basketball and hockey teams. I chased my share of girls. I tried to make lines flow. I acted in plays. But I had teachers like Mr. Addo and Mr. Agbengu who made sure I also paid attention to my studies. Teachers must be given credit when they perform well because they play important roles in making us take advantage of our gifts. I know that all you students here have that wonderful, God-given talent. If you know how good you arc, you will be happy to discover tomorrow how good you can bc. Amen!

Unite or Perish! The Reconciliation Imperative Speech Delivered to the Rotary Club of Kumasi-East

August 17, 1996

I wish to express my sincere appreciation to the Rotary Kumasi-East for the honor of inviting me to share a few thoughts with you this evening. I have chosen the topic "Unite or Perish" not because I am a prophet of doom but because I am a disciple of hope and prosperity. I have spent the past year or so preaching national reconciliation, national government, and unity. I have not succeeded yet. Sometimes those of us reconciliation people are misunderstood and considered naïve, suspicious, or, worse, opportunists.

But it is important to keep talking and doing something to achieve national reconciliation because the lack of it has slowed down our growth and development as a nation. We need a national team and unity of purpose and resolve to achieve accelerated economic and social development in the 1990s.

Almost a year ago, I delivered a speech at the fourth anniversary dinner of the *Ghanaian Chronicle* entitled, "Can the Rawlings Presidency Be Saved?" The storm aroused by my humble attempt to briefly analyze the pros and cons of the Rawlings presidency left me without any doubt that our beloved country Ghana needs healing. Since that night, I have had several discussions about the Rawlings presidency and Rawlings the man. There does not seem to be a middle ground in people's perception and feelings when it comes to J. J. Rawlings. It appears that either you are for or against the man and his presidency. I am not sure that this situation is good for our country.

Ladies and gentlemen, I am convinced that the single biggest issue facing our country Ghana is the division in our society into those for or against government. This division has bred intolerance of opposing views. It has denied those perceived to be against government access to business opportunities. It has denied government the benefit of some of the best talent the country needs to solve its numerous problems in areas such as health, education, and private sector development.

This division has granted automatic entry into business and social opportunities to those perceived to be for government. In some cases, this has led to mediocre results for the nation. Frustration has, on occasion, led talented and ambitious Ghanaian citizens to cause mischief and, worse, to commit economic and social crimes against the nation.

Fear of being victimized has led citizens to hide incomes and send scarce foreign currency abroad for safekeeping. In the final analysis, all of us, for or against government, have suffered from the status of underdevelopment brought about by these actions.

Rotarians and special guests, a year ago, I chose to use the *Ghanaian Chronicle* anniversary dinner to make an important point about polarization of thought and action in Ghana. With your permission, I wish to take advantage of the opportunity you have given me to press home the case for national unity and reconciliation. This time, I hope to make my point clearer in order to minimize confusion and misunderstanding. In case anyone is wondering, the personal difficulties I encountered after the *Chronicle* dinner speech have only strengthened my resolve to work harder to advance the cause of national unity. It has encouraged me to continue to make the case on the need to build a national team for superior results.

Did J. J. Rawlings invent intolerance, polarization, hatred, and political suppression in this country? Did our inability to reach our economic and social potential start with Rawlings? Absolutely not. Please permit me to take a quick look at our history since independence and see what the facts tell us.

Those of you who remember the pre-1966 days know that all was not well in Ghana, particularly after 1960. Ghana became a one-party state. Many opposition politicians and others suspected to be their sympathizers or funding sources were harassed, put in jail, or denied business opportunities. Many fled to exile. Nkrumah's word was the law. People surrounding him engineered a cult following around him. Opposition leaders went around the world to ask the British and Americans not to support development projects in Ghana. Our country was divided. Our development plans faltered.

During the immediate post-1966 period, CPP people were harassed. They were denied jobs and contracts. If you are a CPP man, you will remember the sight of a live human being caged and paraded in the streets of Accra. The National Liberation Council (NLC) military government paved the way for the people who opposed Nkrumah to win power. We were a divided nation. We refused to use the best talent available because some of them had not repented their "CPP or Nkrumah" sins. The Busia government could not implement its programs successfully.

In 1972, another military government came. We had Operation Feed Yourself. The head of that government, General Acheampong, nationalized some enterprises. He took an elephant's share of the Ashanti Goldfields company. Then a craziness called Kalabule took root.

All of a sudden, if your name happened to be "middleman," you were the enemy. Soldiers became businessmen. Young and flexible women were rewarded with nice cars and other things that glittered. There was chaos. Acheampong proposed "Nkabom."

Ghanaians said no to his brand of *nkabom* or union government (UNIGOV). The government fought the people. The electoral commissioner escaped through a window. Those who opposed the UNIGOV idea found themselves in jail. Rumormongering became a crime. Evaporated milk, sardines, and toilet rolls became essential commodities. The decay in our society deepened. Ghana was a divided country. Our economy collapsed.

General Akuffo intervened through a palace coup. The country once again was on its way to another political era. Then came J. J. Rawlings, briefly but with a big bang. He handed over government to President Limann. But his own party's people fought in court. Some even say that he was too harmless. Imagine that!

Then came J. J. Rawlings again. The new Rawlings set for himself the very high standards of probity, accountability, and integrity in public life. Hero or villain, none of us can ignore what we have come to know as "the Rawlings factor." How successful he has been is in the eyes of the beholder. Indeed, many Ghanaians called Nkrumah "Osagyefo" and sang his praises until the day he was overthrown. Many Ghanaians hailed Kotoka, Acheampong, and Rawlings. In the case of J. J. Rawlings, quite a few people participated in singing the "Let the Blood Flow" refrain. I am not here to judge any one of our leaders, past and present.

My point is that, throughout the years, we have been a divided nation. A significant section of our people is always locked in some form of struggle with the leaders. In the fight for freedom, freedom of speech, and power, our collective need to develop our economy and society in general gets left behind. As we all know, without prosperity, it is actually difficult to live in peace. As one Ghanaian singer puts it, "*Kurow mu beye wo dew a, onye wo boto mu.*"

Ladies and gentlemen, I wish to offer a few suggestions on how we can achieve reconciliation. Not too long ago, Bishop Tutu of South Africa suggested something to the effect that, before reconciliation can take place, there is the need to search for truth. He went further to state that there is the need for wrongdoers to repent and ask for forgiveness. Then there is the need for victims to forgive. It will be a great day in Ghana if Ghanaians collectively one day choose to heed these words of wisdom and try to achieve lasting reconciliation.

In the area of truth, we can start by admitting that all of our governments, military and civilian alike, have at some point taken decisions that have alienated some group of citizens.

Some citizens have died in prison. But we the people must also admit that we have played our part in supporting all governments, past and present, even when they denied other citizens the right to freedom and the right to earn a decent living. Some Ghanaians continue to look the other way as long as their needs are taken care of. We forget sometimes that what goes around has the tendency of coming around.

We Ghanaians have chanted, "Nkrumah does no wrong." Then when he was no longer around, we called him a dictator. Some even said he was not a Ghanaian. We cheered when someone said to our creditors, "*Yenntua.*" We supported the Busia government when it expelled our brothers and sisters because they were "aliens." Remember, to some, J. J. used to mean "Junior Jesus." It wasn't Iranians, Americans, or Russians. We Ghanaians supported every one of our leaders. If we want reconciliation, we must admit that none of us has clean hands. We must swallow our collective pride and promise to do better for our country.

To our present leaders, particularly to the ruling government, I have only one simple piece of advice. Make friends for none of us knows what tomorrow might bring. The best way to make friends is to protect the interest of all Ghanaians and not just those who visibly support you. The best way to win the support of businesspeople and professionals is to cultivate their attention by mixing with them and encouraging their economic and professional pursuits with tangible support. Jobs, contracts, licenses, and open doors can work magic.

To the press, I am convinced they can play a significant role in the quest for national reconciliation if they decide to seek only what is best for all Ghanaians. Our press (private or state-owned) has become entrenched in the polarization game. They write, speak, or show news to support only one side, for or against the Rawlings government. They must criticize everyone in a constructive way. They must report all news worth reporting. They must show pictures of everyone who is newsworthy and not only those for or against government.

Ladies and gentlemen, I wish to conclude by asking you to join hands to work hard to unite our country. We must encourage each other to tell the truth, to repent, and to forgive. A divided nation has divided attention. Divided, we cannot accelerate our development because someone from within will always try to disrupt our forward march. I don't need to tell you that the worst enemy is the one from within.

In the competitive world we are in today, nations are competing for scarce global resources. As we talk about becoming a middle-income country by the year 2020, others are planning to become a top-income country by the same year.

We have to pull together with single purpose and best brains available. Otherwise, we will forever remain a nation of missed opportunities and mediocre results.

Divisive politics has polarized our country and prevented us from reaching our potential as a shining star in the world. We have not reached our goal of becoming a strong economically and socially advanced African nation because of it. Can we unite and reconcile? Absolutely. It will be difficult. But we can do it. Can we become a First World country and a prosperous nation? Yes, but we must first learn to live in unity and pull in the same direction. I hope my little contribution tonight will serve the interest of all concerned. Thank you.

To the President of the Republic
Of Ghana, J. J. Rawlings

January 24, 1997

I t is in order to offer congratulations to Mr. Rawlings on his winning
the mandate to lead the nation for four more years. J. A. Kufuor fought
hard. Edward Mahama tried hard. They all deserve our commendation
for having the courage, determination, and will to face the nation and
offer their services for our common good. But this time, the man with
the winning message, resources, programs, and broad appeal is the one
we must now all call President Rawlings. We must all accord him the
respect, support, and encouragement he needs to do the best his talent and
experience will let him for all of us.

Now, the parliamentary and presidential elections are over. The people
have spoken. They have made their choices. Whatever preceded the actual
voting must be regarded as attempts to win the minds and conscience of
voters. Party flags, slogans, symbols, and songs were meant to make the
parties popular. Partisan arguments, debates, and behavior were all part
of demonstrating who had the best programs, message, and vision for
Ghanaians.

Sometimes, it seemed as if the political campaign were a matter of
life and death. Some people used the cover of politics to settle personal
scores. Of course, there were people who brought politics into business and

starved their opponents, real or perceived, of business opportunities. Such behavior belongs to yesterday.

Flying party colors belongs to the period before December 4. Now is the time for flying our national colors. Now that presidential and parliamentary choices have been made, it is important that all of us focus our attention on accelerating the development of our nation. In this regard, I wish to offer my views on our forward march to the man who continues in the position as president of the Republic of Ghana, Mr. J. J. Rawlings.

With this reelection, the president must now feel more secure, confident, and relaxed in his seat as head of state. There is no need to worry about winning or losing an election again. There is no stolen verdict document to contend with. Nor is there a boycott of parliamentary elections to deprive him and the country of useful opposing views and suggestions. The only consideration now is the business of Ghana. As a human being, Mr. Rawlings will want to leave a legacy that historians and future generations will consider favorably.

I suggest he should look to the future, the new four years, and not the past fifteen years for inspiration to lead. As the winner of a hotly contested race, his work will be made easier if he lives by the words and considerate demeanor he showed in his last political broadcast before the election that portrayed the image of an apologetic, welcoming, smiling leader, concerned about the problem of developing the whole country for all of the people.

I wish to suggest the building of a national team for the consideration of the president. In the final days of the campaign to regain the presidency, Mr. Rawlings promised to use the best men and women this country has to offer to move this country forward without regard to their ethnic, religious, or political orientation. This, when implemented, would be one of the best things to happen to this country.

There are excellent men and women in all the political parties who have the interest of the whole nation at heart. There are also many nonpartisan men and women with great talent and national interest. President Rawlings will enhance his appeal and strengthen his grip on the national agenda by choosing a multiparty national government. He can use the results of the elections as a guide in determining how much of opposition and nonpartisan people to select to assist him. He should use whatever method makes him comfortable. Of course, he must be careful to choose people who will put the national interest above partisan objectives. But as president, he has the power to remove anyone who does not prove to be a team player.

Ghanaians should not only ask if the president will agree to appoint opposition people to high public positions. We should also ask if opposition people will also agree to serve in a government led by J. J. Rawlings. It will be a wonderful thing if there is agreement on all sides to enable the building of a true, multiparty national team. I am convinced that, if our politicians' hearts will be big enough to allow the formation of a national team, we can stretch our vision further, we will achieve more, and we will be more united and can accelerate our development as a nation.

I suggest that strengthening our national institutions should be a matter of the highest priority. The vice president, along with a small team of Ghanaian experts, can lead such a project. The vision should be to redesign, reengineer, and renew government not just to seek incremental improvement. Our institutions such as police, customs, tax authorities, immigration, local authorities, and others need significantly overhauled processes, procedures, policies, systems, equipment, and human development. Without strong institutions to execute our plans, our national vision will remain a dream.

Finally, I suggest that the president should establish personal rapport with business leaders and entrepreneurs. He should make developing the private sector his personal mission. If he personally takes interest in private sector development, we will achieve breakthrough results in job creation and productivity hitherto thought impossible. This will earn Ghanaians our ticket to the First World even before the year 2020.

Building a strong, developed country requires all our efforts. Ghanaians have done their part and participated in a peaceful election. The voters have made their choices. They have chosen President Rawlings and his team for four more years of leading this nation. We need to accelerate our development in order to fulfill the promises made by all the parties who contested the election. A nonpartisan national team will take us very far in meeting our national vision. A considerate, confident, and positive leader will earn our respect. A successful, confident, respected nation will result from confident, respected leadership.

Vision for Nation-Building:
An Economist's View "A Mind Is a Terrible Thing to Waste" The University of Education, Winneba

April 23, 1997

I first want to thank the organizers of this event for honoring me with the invitation to share my views on nation-building with you this afternoon. I have chosen what I consider to be an attitudinal subtitle to the suggested topic, "A Mind Is a Terrible Thing to Waste," a well-known theme of the United Negro College Fund, an American organization that promotes education and gives scholarships to African Americans. I am a firm believer in the theme. You have given me this chance to stretch my imagination a little bit, and I hope what I have to offer will justify the trust and confidence you have put in me.

In the years immediately prior to 1957, the then–Gold Coast had one vision, to become an independent nation. On March 6, 1957, the dream became reality. Ghana became an independent country, free from British colonial rule. The leaders of the independence movement wanted "Self-Government Now!" They worked hard and sacrificed much of their personal lives and resources to achieve it. They had a vision and the courage to put their minds to good use for all of us. Thank God, they were successful in making this very important dream a reality. Having a strong clear vision is a powerful weapon that comes from having a fertile mind.

We are now in 1997, forty years after political independence. If we are to discuss a vision for nation-building, we must first take stock of our present or "as is" situation before we talk about the future or the "to be" desired situation.

After forty years of self-government, what do we have? We have recently decided to liberalize our economy and to rely on the private sector. The liberalization has come at a time when many countries in the world have agreed to free their markets and make business opportunities available to all in the world. In this global market, it is a matter of who has competitive advantage or who has the ability to utilize the national core competencies and resources for full benefit. In other words, the countries who are well positioned are the ones to enjoy rapid economic growth and prosperity. The ones who exercise their minds to full advantage are benefiting from the evolution of a global economy.

So let's take stock. We have a lot to offer. Without a doubt, we have natural resources at competitive amounts. It is well known that we have gold, diamond, bauxite, timber, and other resources and world-class levels. We have a beautiful, natural landscape, oceanfront beaches, tropical rainfall pattern, and good vegetation, and we are well located to enjoy maximum sunshine.

Ghana has also been abundantly endowed with talented people. The wonderful Ghanaian talent has shown brilliantly in the international arena in business and public life. Indeed, a Ghanaian can be described as the chairman of the Board of the World. I am referring, of course, to the most honorable Kofi Annan, the secretary-general of the United Nations. Nature has truly blessed us.

But what have we done with this wonderful natural endowment in the past forty years? Since we are having this discussion at an educational institution, let's begin with our educational system. In 1997, after forty years of independence, we still have children who have to carry their own desks and chairs to school so they will have a place to sit and work. Some schools do not have adequate shelter to protect the teachers and students from rain and the other elements. Some schools do not have the full complement of teachers; many do not have the textbooks and equipment required. In several communities, children are being forced to stay at home because their parents cannot afford the cost of education. I do not have to tell you about the situation at the secondary and university levels. You know the problems of poor facilities, crowded dormitories, and lecture halls better than I do. What products do we hope to put on the world market to compete with the ones from the developed economies using our grossly inadequate facilities? First-year students at universities in the United States are using their own personal computers, communicating on the Internet, and receiving lecture materials on electronic media. They have easy access to abundant research databases. All over the country on the education front, our God-given human talent is starting out life at a disadvantage. In many ways, we are wasting the minds we need to develop to dream wonderful dreams for our nation.

On the economic front, the story is not any better. In life, what matters are the results we have to show for our efforts. In our national life of forty years, we have very little to show to the world given the abundant natural resources God has given to this country. Inflation is still running at the 30 to 40 percent level. At least half of labor in this country is unemployed or, at best, underemployed. The situation is worse for junior secondary school (JSS) and senior secondary school (SSS) graduates who have not been able to move to the next educational level.

Unemployment is due to the inability of the private sector to raise productivity. The production problem is also directly linked to the inability of the private sector to gain access to capital at reasonable rates. When banks demand 42 to 50 percent interest on loans granted to the private sector, what legitimate business venture do we expect can be pursued to gain the more than 70 percent return required to break even? Bankers also tell us that government has tied their hands by requiring them to put a very high percentage of deposits into government bonds like treasury bills. When government treasury bills are paying interest around 42 percent, bankers and individuals find it easier to give the monies they have to government instead of the private sector. Government spends; the private sector invests.

The scarcity of reasonable business capital is creating business magicians in this country. Some of the magic being performed is clearly illegal. No country can prosper if businesspeople are driven to believe that they can only thrive by bribing bank managers and government officials and resorting to illegal means of gaining capital and business opportunity. The question is: Are we pushing the private sector to use their God-given minds to do evil?

My purpose was not to bring doom and gloom. Indeed, I do believe that the best days of our nation are ahead of us. So now that we gained some insight into the present situation, what should our vision for nation-building be? What should the future look like? How should we put our minds to good use?

In my mind, the way forward is simple and clear. We should aim to build a First World country in our collective lifetime. This is the only vision our country Ghana can have. We have first-class natural resources. We have first-class talent. We have a first-class geographic environment. God has given us all the tools we need to build a first-class country. And we all know that God does not create second-class citizens. So we must give glory to God by aiming to become first class. None of us will get up and choose to be second or third class in anything. Every soccer player wants to win the World Cup. All boxers want to become world champions. All athletes want to win the ultimate gold medal in the Olympics. As students, you are all aiming for first-class honors in your field of study. Is there anyone here who is aiming for a third-class, lower degree? I don't think so.

My fellow Ghanaians, how can we build a First World country given the fact that we have not managed our natural endowments well?

- We must believe we can become a first-class nation. Our leaders must have this vision and should be able articulate it well and enough to allow all Ghanaians to share it. As the saying goes, "If you dream it, you can reach it." Being First World means seeking excellence in all areas of our national life and rewarding those who excel in their chosen fields.

- We must make economics, not politics, the central area of focus of our nation. We should seek economic advantage for the country and not seek personal political advantage. In this regard, the first priority is to concentrate on job creation. Without jobs, many of our national goals cannot be met. Therefore, all of government's efforts must be channeled to the task of creating jobs, particularly in the private sector. This means that our present program of action with the World Bank and other donors must be channeled through the private sector and must have job creation as the objective. This also means that all available capital, including some capital in the hands of government, must be made available at reasonable interest rates to Ghanaian entrepreneurs for job creation activities. The present social security scheme should be made flexible to encourage the development and growth of private pension schemes. Pension funds in the hands of the productive private sector will be a powerful developmental tool. Ladies and gentlemen, I wish to emphasize that it is only through the creation of good, permanent jobs that our health, education, and housing needs can be met. Without good jobs, Ghanaians cannot afford to pay the fees required by good schools, the best hospitals, and others.

- To become a First World country requires that we agree, as a nation, to honor, cherish, and celebrate success. We should encourage businesspeople who have been able to create jobs to become more successful. Their successes must be visible, and their stories must be told publicly so others may not only share their vision, but more importantly, so others will know that it takes hard work, perseverance, and personal sacrifice to be successful. As Ghanaians, we have become experts at hiding wealth, success, and achievement. "Low profile" is the motto of some of the most law-abiding, successful professionals and businesspeople in Ghana. By making their successes a secret, they help perpetuate the myth that all businesspersons are crooks out to bribe their way, cheat, and only seek personal gain. This behavior has been reinforced by the actions of some in our society who only want to see the wrong in what others do. At this stage in our development, when we review, investigate, probe, and inquire, it should be done with the intent to correct and encourage, not to punish and destroy. We must discourage the behavior of hiding wealth and achievement by making it safe to be successful in Ghana.

- To become a First World country, we must have First World leaders. Our leaders must themselves have a positive view of the ability of Ghanaians to cultivate a strong work ethic and a legitimate private sector. They must be qualified and know what is good in life. Leaders are human beings and, like all of us, limited by their experience and qualifications. More important, their ability to learn limits them. Our leaders, too, must believe that a mind is a terrible thing to waste.

I hope my brief presentation has been worthy of your invitation. I thank you very much for your kind attention.

Considerations toward a Successful Implementation of the Value-Added Tax (VAT) System in Ghana

July 27, 1997

Introduction

The value-added tax (VAT) has become a contentious matter in Ghanaian society in recent years. The last time government attempted to implement the VAT, there was widespread resistance to it, leading to violence and loss of revenue to the state. It also resulted in a permanent arbitrary increase in prices of goods and services in the country. Government had to take the unprecedented decision of withdrawing the VAT after only a few months of its introduction. One reason frequently cited for the failure of the VAT is the lack of adequate preparation (including public education) before introducing the new tax. Preparations are being made for the reintroduction of the VAT. It appears that the government prefers the rate of 15 percent. Some areas of commerce have been considered for exemption from the VAT.

It is not my purpose to argue for or against the VAT this time around. The objective is to present some simple suggestions to be considered by those charged with reviewing the VAT bill to assist them to arrive at a solution that will have a greater chance of achieving success.

Reasons Given for the VAT

Government officials have given a number of reasons for the reintroduction of the VAT. Key among them are:

- Broaden the tax net to cover a greater number of entrepreneurs and enterprises in order to raise more revenue
- Make the system of taxation more equitable
- Comply with an Economic Community of West African States (ECOWAS) requirement that all West African economies harmonize their systems of taxation through the implementation of the VAT system of taxation

It is important to consider the key reasons advanced for the reintroduction of the VAT carefully before final touches are put on the VAT bill placed before Parliament and certainly before firm plans are made for the new tax system's implementation. Those charged with the implementation of the VAT can be successful if the right equipment and software are found and accepted for its introduction. This way, what is designed for implementation will have good rationale, particularly when it comes time to prepare the public to comply with the requirements of the new system.

If we accept in Ghana that the present government tells us that we are operating under a market-based economy and one that is to rely on the private sector for growth and development, then there are valid reasons to review some of the reasons given for the reintroduction of the VAT.

Equity cannot be the basis for the VAT. VAT is a tax on consumption even though much is made of the value that the producer of goods and services is supposed to add. Ghana is a consumer nation. Unlike a country like Nigeria with several big producers of goods and services to make the implementation of VAT successful even when the majority of the population avoids it, Ghana has a small number of overtaxed producers. The consumers who happen to be in the majority are also a relatively poor population. Therefore, a tax on consumption as the VAT will affect the majority of Ghanaians much more since they will pay the same rate as the well-to-do for the most basic of products and services.

The VAT cannot be introduced on the basis of raising more revenue. Most revenue is currently coming from the formal, private sector, particularly those in manufacturing and financial goods and services areas. The enterprises in these areas are currently overburdened with high interest rates and high overhead and suffer from low profits. A tax to make their goods and services more expensive in an economy that is experiencing low growth will not raise more revenue, at least not from the sale of goods produced in this country.

The introduction of the VAT on the basis of broadening the tax net can only be justified if the collection system associated with it is designed and implemented to be more efficient than what pertains in the present situation. This will mean finding new ways of collecting tax from the informal sector, which makes up the majority of workers and commercial enterprises in the country. The informal sector uses low technology and often does not have accounting records that can be relied upon to measure their tax performance. This problem in itself should not prevent anyone from paying the tax levied.

However, the point being made here is that the problem of how to broaden the tax base is there to be solved, VAT or no VAT. Innovative ways must be found through the introduction of the VAT to make this happen.

VAT complicates the entire tax collection system. Therefore, to be successful, a lot more effort has to be expended to achieve effectiveness and efficiency in the tax administration system itself. If the system is not improved with better procedures, systems, and information technology, administering the VAT itself will become so burdensome as to prevent government to achieve the goal of broadening the tax net to find more payers.

A factor to be considered that is related to the revenue objective is the VAT rate to be charged. I can appreciate the fact that the service/sales tax charged by enterprises like hotels is 15 percent. This has probably influenced the proposal to charge a VAT rate of 15 percent, presumably so as not to lose revenue presently being collected. If the present service tax rate has been an important consideration, then the matter should be looked at again. We should not overburden all enterprises just because we do not want to lose revenue that a segment of the business community is paying. The volume of activity in some business sectors will go down. One needs to visit the case of the automobile super tax to realize that a higher tax leads to a decrease in business activity for the enterprises affected, which then causes a further depression in the overall economy. Lower tax rates encourage investment, lead to more economic activity, and, in fact, generate more revenue for government!

There is also the thorny issue of whether we should be giving more revenue to the government sector when all indicators point to the need to reduce overall government expenditure. If the effort being put into the VAT matter is applied to the task of reducing government expenditure, this economy should "take off," as President Rawlings has been known to project on a few occasions. International observers and analysts have suggested that government over the past ten years has successfully raised revenue by more than a factor of three. The unfortunate fact is that expenditure over the same period has exceeded the significantly increased revenue.

The need to implement the VAT system to comply with ECOWAS requirements is an important reason to consider. If this is a significant, compelling factor, then government should be able to educate the public on the benefits that come from being a good member of ECOWAS.

Suggestions

If there are good reasons for implementing the VAT, then it must be made an effective tax by designing it in such a way as to make it possible for the public to comply with its requirements:

- VAT or no VAT, the systems associated with the collection of government tax must be made more efficient and effective. A uniform, single national identification system could make business registration information available for use by the tax authorities, and this should increase their effectiveness. In the age of super computers and Internet, it is imperative that the tax authorities have the best information technology available to use in achieving efficiency. The suggestion is that, the more efficient and effective the system of administration is, the broader the tax net will become, VAT or no VAT.

- The VAT rate can be varied by industry segment so those who are used to collecting the 15 percent service tax on behalf of government already can continue to work with that same rate. However, those who are not used to collecting this type of tax on behalf of government and will have to charge an additional amount than usual on their goods and services can be allowed to charge a minimal rate in the order to 3 to 5 percent. Once again, it has been proven elsewhere that, the lower the rate, the greater the rate of compliance.

- The VAT can be implemented in a phased manner to improve the chance of success. A number of enterprises or industry segments can be phased in over a three- to five-year time frame to increase the chance of success. This way, implementation can begin with the ones already used to collecting tax on behalf of government using the rates they are currently charging.

"A Great, Free, and Caring Society" Speech Given at the Tenth Anniversary Celebration Dinner of the *Independent* Newspaper

May 7, 1999

I wish to thank the publisher of the *Independent* for the invitation to speak at this important anniversary celebration. I am a believer in celebrating important events in life. So I appreciate the opportunity to take part in your celebration.

One important event in the life of organizations and individuals is achievement or success. Success is important in life. But success is hard to come by. Everyone wants it. But not everyone is able or willing to persevere, work hard, sacrifice, and provide the service or deliver the product necessary to become successful. Indeed, in business life and a newspaper is a business, most people fail to achieve the longevity that is a requirement for success. In general, most businesses (a good 60 to 75 percent of them worldwide) fail within twelve months of their initiation. Some hang on as businesses in name only for a while but eventually fail to make any positive impact on their clientele or on their own pocketbooks.

Ladies and gentlemen, in Ghana, many newspapers have come and gone. But the *Independent* has managed to be here for a decade. Longevity is not necessarily the most meaningful yardstick in business or even in life. But in our Ghanaian environment where the state-owned newspapers have been dominant for so long, ten years of being in business for a private newspaper is a mark to be celebrated.

For a newspaper to be considered truly successful, not only must it have long life, it must also be respected. It must make a positive impact on national life. I am happy to tell the publisher, the editorial staff, and all personnel of the *Independent* that you have become successful in your industry. You are respected, and you have made a positive impact on our national life here in Ghana. Please accept my congratulations for your perseverance, hard work, and a job well done.

Ladies and gentlemen, these are not just nice words. Let me give you one concrete example of the impact this newspaper is making. Commerce these days is thriving on the Internet. On the New York Stock Exchange, technology stocks, particularly those companies that provide services through the Internet, have become the stocks to watch. For those of us who travel often, the newspapers we read are the newspapers on the Internet. In this regard, the *Online Independent* has become part of the daily routine for many Ghanaians in North America and Europe.

Other Ghanaian newspapers are on the Internet. But the *Online Independent* is regular and timely. The first thing many Ghanaians abroad do when they get up in the morning on Tuesdays and Thursdays is to find the *Online Independent* so they can read about what is making news in Ghana. So for them, the *Independent* shapes what they do and think about their home country twice a week. You have made them closer to home. Once again, accept my congratulations for making a positive impact in your chosen profession.

In 1995, I accepted an invitation to speak at an anniversary dinner of the *Ghanaian Chronicle*. I spoke on the pros and cons of the Rawlings presidency. Some people harassed me after the event because of the content of my speech. Others harassed me greatly, including a government minister who nearly physically attacked me at a restaurant, not for what I said, but because I had spoken at a *Ghanaian Chronicle* public event, identifying myself with the enemy and the opposition. The word in certain influential circles in government after the speech was that I was an owner of the *Ghanaian Chronicle*! Imagine that!

Well, here I am, almost four years later, at another anniversary dinner for yet another private newspaper. To the respected business leader in Ghana who told me after the *Ghanaian Chronicle* dinner speech, "Young man, you must have just arrived in the country. Don't you know that we here only talk about this man in private?" No, I am not here to evaluate the Rawlings presidency again. Once is enough. To the influential government officials who may want to know, no, I do not own shares in the *Independent*. To the *Daily Graphic* people who may be wondering, yes, I am available to speak at your anniversary dinner!

I am here, and I was at the *Ghanaian Chronicle* dinner because I believe in the freedom of the press. I am convinced that when the press is free so are the rest of us. When the press is silenced, so are we. I do have my own complaints from time to time about the quality of the information the press (both state-owned and private) sometimes puts out. Sometimes you make mistakes that are costly to others. But you are a necessary part of our Ghanaian life. So you need to be encouraged to do your job better. You need to be supported to play your role diligently, accurately, and without official impediments.

It is in this regard that I wish all political parties would agree to repeal our criminal libel laws and agree to pass a Freedom of Information Act in Parliament so the press can do the job this society needs them to do. I am here this evening to plead with you to help create a great, free, and caring Ghanaian society in the next millennium.

Over the past three decades, our governments have steered the affairs of state in a direction where we now find that the value of a Ghanaian human being is determined by:

- whether he or she supports the ruling party
- if he or she has parents who have enough money to afford private schools
- if he or she has enough money to pay cash before consultation and treatment locally or to be sent overseas for medical care

- if the private sector is generous enough to provide support
- if a donor agency or an nongovernmental organization (NGO) has funds to support a project.

Government has increasingly ceased to be the caretaker and the caregiver. The privatization of the entire Ghanaian society needs to be interrupted and fast before we all become selfish, uncaring citizens. It is for these and other reasons that I wish to place a significant burden on you, the press, here tonight.

In world history, both ancient and modern, great societies have often been described as the ones that allowed their citizens to create wealth. Some had great armies that conquered others and created empires that stretched across oceans. I am not talking about those great societies. I am referring to great societies that accept to free their citizens to pursue life in liberty and not to live in fear of the state. Great societies take care of the poor and disadvantaged. Great societies give the poor hope and encouragement to strive to overcome their problems. Great societies encourage their citizens to create wealth to be shared and do not destroy what others have struggled to build.

Great societies celebrate the success of their citizens because they know that, by using those who have become successful as good role models, others can also have hope and strive to achieve. Only when we have good, positive role models can the youth be encouraged to do the right things. Great societies are peaceful nations and have civil governments that believe in the supremacy of the rule of law and not the might and power of being the ruler. Great societies have leaders who, like the citizens they govern, do not hold them in contempt. Great societies have leaders who reach out often to guide, counsel, encourage, and lift people up when they fall or fail because they know the successes of the citizens are their successes. The leaders of great societies measure their successes by how many lives they have improved, not destroyed, during their tenure.

In my humble opinion, we have not built a great society in Ghana. My challenge to the publisher, the editorial staff, and other employees of the *Independent*; the private press in general; and the state-owned media as a whole is to use your positions of influence to help make this country a great society in the next millennium. My challenge comes in four areas: believe in yourself, be nonpartisan in your work, help create wealth and reduce poverty, and help reconcile our people.

- If you in the media are going to help make Ghana a great society in the next millennium, you must first believe that you are important, needed, and have the influence needed to make change happen. If you are not sure of who you are, let me remind you. You are without a doubt an important, needed, and influential component of our society. What you write can help people. What you write can also hurt people. I challenge you to choose to investigate and write about news and stories that help our society. Ghanaian people believe what they read in the newspaper. They like to read. They like news, and like any other people in the world, they like to read stories about people who matter in the country. You should feed this need, but you must choose to do it in a way that encourages the other influential people in this country to do what is required to make us a great, free, and caring society.

- You must try as hard as possible to be nonpartisan. The reality of the newspaper situation in Ghana is that the state-owned media mostly follows the line of government. When that happens, the government in power wins, but the Ghanaian society loses. The reality of today is also that the private press mostly follows the line of opposition to government. When that happens, the opposition gains points, but the Ghanaian society loses. My point is that our newspapers must criticize government when it fails, but they must also encourage government by giving it credit when it succeeds. It sounds simple. But the extremely partisan reality of politics in Ghana over the past two decades makes this a difficult task for both the private and state-owned press. But if we are to become a great society in the next millennium, we need a nonpartisan, well-balanced press at least most of the time.

- Great societies develop men and women who risk their capital to create wealth so the rest can have a share in it. But we cannot create or share wealth if we seek to destroy the few men and women in Ghana who dare to risk their capital to build enterprises that create jobs and produce goods and services. All parts of the press, public and private, must resist the urge to brand every businessperson who appears successful an enemy of labor, a cheat, a thief, a cocaine dealer, or a friend of government. The public needs education about the difficulties and rewards that come with doing business in Ghana. Our youth must be shown role models who have succeeded not because of political or government contacts and government contracts, but by being the best through their hard work, great personal sacrifice, and perseverance. Ladies and gentlemen, I believe that God is a kind God. He did not put us Africans on this earth to suffer and die. And so I consider poverty a disease that must be understood and cured and not a condition to be glorified and made permanent. We will not cure the poverty disease if we kill the spirit of those who can create wealth for others in our society to share. You in the media should lead the crusade to make our society great by pointing out what we do wrong that entrenches poverty and by also highlighting what we do successfully to reduce poverty.

- We should make our society a peaceful one. When foreigners compare us to countries like Sierra Leone, Liberia, Rwanda, Congo, and others, we appear a very peaceful country. We appear to be an island of stability and calm. But so did Yugoslavia when the Soviet Union was intact. Before the Northern Conflict and the alleged vanishing genitals who would have thought that Ghanaians could also kill each other so easily? Let's face the ugly truth. We are not at peace with each other in this country. You can help bring peace to our people by writing stories that will heal and reconcile our people instead of the ones that open and reopen old wounds. You and I know that we have some very big and ugly old wounds that should be kept closed.

Ladies and gentlemen, our newspapers seem to like stories with the name Rawlings in it. Anytime I see a screaming headline with that name in it, I ask journalists, both public and private, why they have this seeming fetish. Usually they tell me that the name Rawlings and the actions of the president and his wife sell papers. The state-owned press covers everything involving the president and his wife and government ministers. Television cameras often will not move to cover any event unless the president, his wife, (these days, the vice president and his wife), or government ministers are involved. When they leave, the cameras leave. Do we only matter when we become part of government? Don't you think actions like these make our people overvalue being in government?

Please allow me to test your level of tolerance. We all know that the members of the Rawlings family are also human beings. Not so? As human beings, I am sure they do get tired of all the stories, both the positive and the negative ones. Can't you imagine Nana Konadu taking J. J. to task after one of those speeches he sometimes makes that sell private newspapers? Do they really deserve to be criticized all the time?

And do they really deserve to be praised all the time? If a Ghanaian president is to become the human being we all know he or she is, the press can help show the way. Can both the private and the state-owned media start by treating President Rawlings like a human being? To put it another way, can we create a monster and expect him or her to show human mercies and compassion? I ask you, is it too late to start treating J. J. Rawlings, the man who has become the most dominant personality in Ghana for the past two decades, as the human being he is?

When the press pays all the attention to government officials, it means that other important business, social, and political leaders and events are ignored. A sad angle to this is that there are other politicians who may unfortunately think that, when they come to power, they will also get all the attention and starve the opposition of news coverage. As is said sometimes, "You do me, I do you." Unfortunately, when politicians take revenge on each other, the whole society suffers. This does not help the cause of reconciliation. I am asking that we don't do to others the negative things they have done us.

Let me test your tolerance level further. Our society should practice reconciliation even when those who have offended us do not appear to have the intention to repent any time soon. It is very difficult for those who have been offended by the various liberation, redemption, revolution, and so forth governments to forgive or seek reconciliation. But as a civil society, we must ask and keep asking for forgiveness.

One thing to me is clear. The J. J. Rawlings era is over. It is on its last legs. Come January 2001, someone whose last name is not Rawlings will be the president of the Republic of Ghana. So why threaten the man at this last hour with bazookas and AK-47s? And lastly, I saw how Dr. Limann lived as a former president. He was someone who had neither been accused nor convicted of corruption, murder, or even arrogance. What happened to him is making good people who would make great leaders reluctant to play active roles in politics. We need to resettle all our former presidents and their families well, including J. J. Rawlings, to prove to ourselves that we Ghanaians are a peaceful people who deserve good leaders and are prepared to make sure that the service they give is well rewarded. What we do for Rawlings will set the tone for the future.

Once again, I ask you not to think about the past but to the next millennium and the great society we will create if we actively work to reconcile our people.

Ladies and gentlemen, the leaders of great societies measure their successes by how many lives they improve during their tenure. We do not have a great society in Ghana. We need to build a great society that is free and caring in the next millennium for all citizens. We need to create wealth that can be shared. We need leaders who will encourage our people to dream and aspire to greatness. We need leaders who will help them build and not tear down so we can cure the poverty problem. We must make our society a peaceful one by reconciling our people.

You ladies and gentlemen of the press are an important, influential part of our society. Use your influence and the opportunities available to you to help make ours a great, free, and caring society in the next century.

To the publisher, the editorial staff, and all employees of the *Independent*, I congratulate you for ten years of being relevant and making a positive difference in your society. I am happy for your success. I wish you well. And I am sincerely grateful for the opportunity to be here tonight. Thank you.

The District Assembly: An Imperative for Change to Enhance Local Development and Grassroots Democracy

September 9, 1999

The establishment of a decentralized local government system in the country is an important and critical one that will decide the ability of the nation to achieve an appreciable level of prosperity. Ghana is largely a rural, poor country with the majority of the people dependent on small-scale or subsistence business activities. In this regard, reducing poverty significantly will require the development of the rural economy. The main agent for change and development in the rural areas is the District Assembly. For this reason, the nature and performance of the District Assembly is important and deserves careful review from a variety of perspectives. The ability of our rural economy to develop depends upon the ability of the District Assembly to lead and facilitate economic development.

At the inception of the present local government system, constitutional multiparty democracy did not exist in the country. Therefore, it made good sense to have a nonpartisan District Assembly. The head of state was also given the right to appoint 30 percent of the members of the Assembly in part to ensure that skills and expertise needed are added where necessary.

This right was to also make it possible to vary the mix of assembly members to reflect gender and other desirable characteristics of the districts.

The inception of the local government system has yielded some positive benefits:

- It has encouraged local communities to take more responsibility for the development of their own areas.
- It has made possible community-based prioritization of development projects.
- It has assisted in promoting the concept of communal action.
- It has also made it possible for a number of people to participate in the democratic process by competing and serving as assembly members.

However, the local government system as is practiced prevents the realization of the intended local development and grassroots democracy benefits. The current local government system requires modification to make it consistent with the current democratic process in the country. More important, it needs modification to make local officials directly accountable to the district community and, as a result, enhance grassroots political development. It also needs modification in order to accelerate the alleviation of rural poverty and promote wealth building. The purpose of this brief paper is to promote the following important changes to the present local government system:

- Remove the right of the president to appoint members to the District Assembly. Ensure the people in the district elect all members of the District Assembly.
- Remove the right of the president to appoint the District Chief Executive. Ensure the people in the district directly elect all district chief executives.
- Remove the nonpartisan requirement of District Assembly elections. Ensure the right of political parties to field and support candidates for election to the District Assembly.

An objective analysis of the current situation supports the need for these modifications. I have had the opportunity to experience the current situation from a firsthand level through my participation in last year's District Assembly elections and by serving currently as the assembly member for the Akotobinsin electoral area of the Komenda-Edina-Eguafo-Abrem (KEEA) District Assembly. As this is just one man's view, I wish to encourage others (Parliament, the press, universities, government, NGOs, and so forth) to examine the current situation to test my conclusions and the need to modify the current local government laws as suggested by me.

The continued appointment of people by the president to the District Assembly is not consistent with our present constitutional and democratic dispensation and does not promote active grassroots participation in the local government system. It promotes, as the president says, mentality that prevents local people from questioning the activities and programs of the Assembly. Government appointees tend in many instances to become appendages or part of the central government's power structure. Therefore, they attempt to wield unnecessary influence on the actions of the Assembly in a way that silences local expression of need, dissatisfaction, and interest.

Democracy depends upon the expression of choice by voting. Many critical decisions of the Assembly require a two-thirds majority. Therefore, with 30 percent of the members appointed by government, it is very difficult for a local community to make decisions that go against the wishes of central government. Given the policy of decentralization and the accepted need to ensure grassroots democracy, the local people who live in the area must be allowed to take precedence over the wishes of nonresidents who happen to be in central government. When the people are involved in decision-making processes at the local level and can see the positive impact of their participation, they tend to take more responsibility for the effects of governance.

When they are removed from the process, they tend not to care about accountability and bad governance. The present situation encourages the latter situation.

As a result of central government's influence on the District Assembly through the appointment of 30 percent of the members, it is very common to find that the wishes of the central government influence subcommittee chairpersons and presiding member elections. Matters of performance and discipline relating to important positions such as subcommittee chairpersons and chief executive require two-thirds majority votes.

When people realize they cannot change the situation no matter how bad, then they tend to stop trying to even attempt to do good things, feeling that any such moves may be frustrated or rejected by the majority government's controlled block of votes. When this happens, the local people lose good ideas, good people and, with it, development opportunities.

The president nominates district chief executives; the District Assembly confirms or rejects them. Unless there are other candidates with favor from the central government, it is virtually impossible to reject the appointment of someone who is not liked or acceptable to the electorate. They do not have the opportunity to indicate their preference. The Assembly finds it difficult to reject the appointment of an incumbent chief executive who has even shown in previous years to be intolerant, ineffective, and/or not generally suitable for the job. Opposition to such a nomination is seen as opposition to the ruling party and the president, even though the Assembly is supposed to be nonpartisan. The district chief executive, in this regard, becomes even more entrenched in loyalty to central government. This makes the person naturally responsive to direction and influence from the center and unresponsive to requests, suggestions, and complaints from the locals.

It should be understood that it is not just that the chief executive himself/herself would necessarily choose to listen to central government over the electorate. Central government itself makes it necessary for the chief executive to consider local views secondary to that of what comes from Accra. The clear impression and perhaps direction is given for the chief executive to know that the position is owed to central government leadership. He or she is asked to support government and party programs, policies, and events, both with time and financial resources. The chief executive, in this regard, becomes the spokesperson and lead person for political actions and strategy at the local level. Since the position is not subject to the wishes of the local people, party positions that conflict with the wishes of the locals tend to be promoted.

By law, District Assembly elections are supposed to be nonpartisan. Political parties are not allowed to sponsor candidates or mount political platforms to support them. Individual candidates are not even allowed to mount their own personal platforms to reduce the influence of money in the campaigns. The electoral commission mounts platforms that all candidates use at the same time to interact with the electorate. On paper, the law has not only good intent but should encourage participation by many in the local community.

In reality, District Assembly elections have become very partisan in nature and practice. I was witness to the fact that political parties sponsored candidates by paying for posters and photographs and engaging in door-to-door and small group campaigning. In some instances, monies were given to the candidates to win support. District chief executives participated in this partisan activity.

Some candidates were introduced privately as government candidates who would be able to use their connections with central government to bring development to their areas. In many electoral areas, it was clear who the government candidate was and who represented the opposition. It must be pointed out that, in some instances, the candidates had enough personal appeal to transcend government and opposition party politics.

After the last Assembly and Unit Committee elections, some district chief executives wrote reports to Accra to show how well they had done by ensuring that the party in power controlled their Assemblies. The ensuing elections for presiding member and subcommittee positions were also controlled to ensure that members considered to be on the side of the party in power won.

The effect of all of this is very clear. While by law, decentralization of power and governance is taking place, but in reality, central government still controls us. But the backdoor control of local government through the appointment of the district chief executive, assembly members, and patronage by central government has made the District Assembly a partisan entity. Some current district chief executives complain that moves made by disgruntled local residents and people with influence with central government to remove them threaten their positions. They complain that they make mistakes because they are nervous about stability of their tenure of office since they could be removed at any time the president is not pleased with their performance. Their nervousness can only be cured with excellent performance in office. However, the ultimate cure will be excellent performance and the satisfaction of their local residents expressed through the ballot box.

The partisan nature or the central government control of the District Assembly is a big hindrance to development. Local businesses, farmers, fishermen, and other entrepreneurs are more easily influenced, ignored, or threatened by a district chief executive who has central government backing and has several billion cedis of resources at his or her disposal.

An elected district chief executive and assembly member will feel the need to consult with the local electorate, understand local priorities, and promote local businesses and social causes because, sooner or later, he or she will have to account to them for continued stay in office. Some well-qualified and experienced men and women have stayed away from offering themselves as candidates for the District Assembly because they do not want to be involved in the battles that frequently go on between government appointees and elected members over priorities and spending matters.

In summary, it is necessary to modify the laws governing District Assemblies because the present provisions that allow the president to appoint the district chief executive and 30 percent of assembly members do not promote accountability of the Assembly to the local people who are most affected by its actions.

The political environment we are now in favors direct accountability of the executive and the legislature to the voters. If this is good for national government, it is also good for local government. Our young democracy needs to encourage the participation of people to have faith and confidence in government so they can play an active part in economic and social development. The best form of participation is the ability to choose who should represent you in government. Those who must do a good job to be allowed to continue to represent the people tend to listen to the needs and priorities of the voters. Therefore, it is important that the people of Ghana be given the opportunity to directly elect all District Assembly members and the district chief executive.

What Happened?

I can say confidently that coming back to Ghana has made me a better person in more ways than one. I have made valuable contributions in both the private and public sectors. I have created jobs in all the ten regions of Ghana. My children have done well and attended good schools, and I am sure they are well on the way to live rewarding lives. But I have been tested in ways I never thought possible or necessary. Members of my immediate family, my wife, and children especially have had to bear the brunt of the personal attacks and threats against my businesses. This is all because of the nervousness of people in government about my participation in politics. What they do not understand is that if, they had not sought to discredit me and strip me of the businesses I had worked hard to establish, I might not have chosen to run for political office. I was satisfied working as a successful international management consultant and entrepreneur. My businesses were profitable and credible, and I had gained the attention of many in the country who sought me out to speak to various organizations. Many prominent business leaders sought my advice. I maintained residence in the United States as well since I had investments there and children in American universities. I am thankful to God that I had a good life and an excellent family life that prevented me from becoming bitter in the face of the daunting challenge of personal attacks launched the ruling NDC party's administration with cooperation from certain individuals from the security agencies. I could have packed up and left Ghana, but I didn't.

After the attack launched on me by government in 1996, I became a public figure, known to many people. The publicity that came with it made people more curious to learn more about me. When many realized who I was, an employer working to make an honest living while giving jobs to hundreds of Ghanaians, someone who had come back home to create jobs outside the capital city Accra where others will not go, I earned a lot of admirers. The government attack backfired. It did not work because my affairs were in order. I had diligently filed my tax returns every year. I had stayed away for the most part from government business and consultancies. I was prepared to earn my living from domestic and international business organizations and individuals using world-class methods and qualified personnel.

Yes, you can come back home to Africa. But it is important to be prepared for the petty jealousies of nervous governments and their business and political followers who are prepared to pull their imagined opponents down.

As it turns out, the political party under whose administration I was subjected to harassment and investigation of fraud and business became unpopular and lost the 2000 elections. I contested the 2000 elections as a candidate to become a member of Parliament. I was subsequently appointed a minister of state and served for six and a half years as minister for economic planning and regional cooperation, minister of energy, and minister of public sector reform. Part III of this series of articles, essays, and speeches will present what happened during the period 2000 to 2008.

About the Author

D r. Papa Kwesi Nduom became a partner in the Milwaukee, Wisconsin, office of Deloitte & Touche, the international public accounting and management consulting firm, in 1986. He was the first African-born professional to achieve that level of success. He moved his practice from Washington, DC, to Africa, where he became director of Deloitte's management consulting practice and head of the West Africa company. He subsequently became chairman of the board of directors of Deloitte & Touche Africa region. He gave all of it up to become a minister of state in Ghana and subsequently a member of Parliament.

He persevered through attempts by the government of Ghana to smear his name through allegations that local and international organizations and individuals resisted. The government agency used for this purpose subsequently dropped its investigations. This did not stop him. It also did not stop those who wanted to find any means at all to stop him from holding public office. He became the member of Parliament for the Komenda-Edina-Eguafo-Abrem constituency. He served as minister of state in the Economic Planning and Regional Cooperation, Energy, and Public Sector portfolios from 2001 to 2007. He also served as chairman of the National Development Planning Commission and the Millennium Development Authority.

Dr. Nduom and his wife, Yvonne, have developed businesses in the hospitality, ICT, financial, and real estate industries with over two thousand employees in Ghana.

This is a continuation of telling his story of going back home through speeches, newspaper articles, and letters written by him.